AF781044

CONTENTS

JUNE 30, 2005

OPENING STATEMENT

WITNESSES

LETTERS, STATEMENTS, ETC., SUBMITTED FOR THE HEARING

APPENDIX

Material Submitted for the Hearing Record

TERRORIST DEATH PENALTY ENHANCEMENT ACT OF 2005, AND THE STREAMLINED PROCEDURES ACT OF 2005

HEARING

BEFORE THE

SUBCOMMITTEE ON CRIME, TERRORISM, AND HOMELAND SECURITY

OF THE

COMMITTEE ON THE JUDICIARY
HOUSE OF REPRESENTATIVES

ONE HUNDRED NINTH CONGRESS

FIRST SESSION

ON

H.R. 3060 and H.R. 3035

JUNE 30, 2005

Serial No. 109–46

Printed for the use of the Committee on the Judiciary

Available via the World Wide Web: http://judiciary.house.gov

U.S. GOVERNMENT PRINTING OFFICE

22–189 PDF WASHINGTON : 2005

For sale by the Superintendent of Documents, U.S. Government Printing Office
Internet: bookstore.gpo.gov Phone: toll free (866) 512–1800; DC area (202) 512–1800
Fax: (202) 512–2250 Mail: Stop SSOP, Washington, DC 20402–0001

COMMITTEE ON THE JUDICIARY

F. JAMES SENSENBRENNER, Jr., Wisconsin, *Chairman*

HENRY J. HYDE, Illinois
HOWARD COBLE, North Carolina
LAMAR SMITH, Texas
ELTON GALLEGLY, California
BOB GOODLATTE, Virginia
STEVE CHABOT, Ohio
DANIEL E. LUNGREN, California
WILLIAM L. JENKINS, Tennessee
CHRIS CANNON, Utah
SPENCER BACHUS, Alabama
BOB INGLIS, South Carolina
JOHN N. HOSTETTLER, Indiana
MARK GREEN, Wisconsin
RIC KELLER, Florida
DARRELL ISSA, California
JEFF FLAKE, Arizona
MIKE PENCE, Indiana
J. RANDY FORBES, Virginia
STEVE KING, Iowa
TOM FEENEY, Florida
TRENT FRANKS, Arizona
LOUIE GOHMERT, Texas

JOHN CONYERS, Jr., Michigan
HOWARD L. BERMAN, California
RICK BOUCHER, Virginia
JERROLD NADLER, New York
ROBERT C. SCOTT, Virginia
MELVIN L. WATT, North Carolina
ZOE LOFGREN, California
SHEILA JACKSON LEE, Texas
MAXINE WATERS, California
MARTIN T. MEEHAN, Massachusetts
WILLIAM D. DELAHUNT, Massachusetts
ROBERT WEXLER, Florida
ANTHONY D. WEINER, New York
ADAM B. SCHIFF, California
LINDA T. SÁNCHEZ, California
CHRIS VAN HOLLEN, Maryland
DEBBIE WASSERMAN SCHULTZ, Florida

Philip G. Kiko, *General Counsel-Chief of Staff*
Perry H. Apelbaum, *Minority Chief Counsel*

Subcommittee on Crime, Terrorism, and Homeland Security

HOWARD COBLE, North Carolina, *Chairman*

DANIEL E. LUNGREN, California
MARK GREEN, Wisconsin
TOM FEENEY, Florida
STEVE CHABOT, Ohio
RIC KELLER, Florida
JEFF FLAKE, Arizona
MIKE PENCE, Indiana
J. RANDY FORBES, Virginia
LOUIE GOHMERT, Texas

ROBERT C. SCOTT, Virginia
SHEILA JACKSON LEE, Texas
MAXINE WATERS, California
MARTIN T. MEEHAN, Massachusetts
WILLIAM D. DELAHUNT, Massachusetts
ANTHONY D. WEINER, New York

Jay Apperson, *Chief Counsel*
Elizabeth Sokul, *Special Counsel for Intelligence and Homeland Security*
Michael Volkov, *Deputy Chief Counsel*
Jason Cervenak, *Full Committee Counsel*
Bobby Vassar, *Minority Counsel*

TERRORIST DEATH PENALTY ENHANCEMENT ACT OF 2005, AND THE STREAMLINED PROCEDURES ACT of 2005

THURSDAY, JUNE 30, 2005

HOUSE OF REPRESENTATIVES,
SUBCOMMITTEE ON CRIME, TERRORISM,
AND HOMELAND SECURITY
COMMITTEE ON THE JUDICIARY,
Washington, DC.

The Subcommittee met, pursuant to notice, at 1 p.m., in Room 2141, Rayburn House Office Building, the Honorable Howard Coble (Chair of the Subcommittee) presiding.

Mr. COBLE. Good afternoon, ladies and gentlemen. The hearing will come to order.

I have good news and bad news. The good news is we are all here in place. The bad news is, Mr. Scott, I am told that there will be a series of votes imminently, so we will play that by ear and then play that card which was dealt to us.

Before I give my opening statement, and before I recognize Mr. Scott, much interest has been indicated in this issue, and some Members of the Subcommittee have requested a second hearing, and we will in fact conduct a second hearing. I'm not sure when that will be, but there will be a second hearing conducted.

I want to welcome everyone to this hearing on the death penalty in America. The issue of the death penalty in our country continues to spark significant debate. The American people believe in the death penalty, especially for terrorists—strike that. Many American people believe in the death penalty, especially for terrorists who have killed Americans. I am convinced that we must be vigilant in ensuring that capital punishment is meted out fairly against those truly guilty criminals.

In the last session of Congress we enacted the Justice for All Act, a far-reaching measure which provided additional safeguards of our death penalty system for post-conviction DNA testing of evidence and improvements in our capital counsel system. This was a matter you all remember that was co-sponsored by our Chairman of the full Committee, Mr. Sensenbrenner, and Mr. Delahunt. And I think, Bobby, you co-sponsored it as well, or did you? The DNA. And Mr. Scott and I were co-sponsors of that as well.

The integrity of our criminal justice system, and in particular our death penalty system, has been enhanced by the enactment of this measure. Despite these improvements, some death penalty opponents continue to argue that the system is broken and that the death penalty system is unfair.

I am concerned about the manner in which the debate is being conducted in some instances. Some death penalty opponents have, in some cases, used some disinformation or even deceptive information on occasion to suggest that the death penalty in our country is not accurate. Yet no credible evidence has been provided, known to me, to suggest that a single innocent person has been executed since the Supreme Court imposed the heightened protections in 1976.

We now have in place greater safeguards and technologies to ensure accuracy at the most important phase of a prosecution; that is, the trial. Aside from the protection of the public and the just punishment of the guilty, our death penalty system vindicates the rights of victims and their families to see that justice is in fact done.

Often during the debate of the death penalty the rights of victims and their need for closure is minimized, or in some instances ignored.

Today we are also examining two important proposals, the first introduced by Representative Carter, the gentleman from Texas, a former Member of the Judiciary Committee. H.R. 3060, the "Terrorist Death Penalty Enhancement Act of 2005," adds the death penalty for a number of terrorist attacks, including weapons of mass destruction, atomic bombs, guerrilla violence, missiles, and other means of attack. The House passed many of these provisions in the last session of Congress, but they were dropped during the conference with the Senate on the Intelligence Reform bill.

In addition, Representative Carter's bill proposes to treat terrorism crimes similarly under our Federal death penalty statute to espionage and treason crimes where a terrorist crime creates a grave risk of harm to our country.

Today we are also examining Representative Lungren's proposal, H.R. 3035, the "Streamlined Procedures Act of 2005," which reforms habeas corpus review of State court convictions.

The Subcommittee in the judicial security hearing, and in examining child crimes, and even last Congress during consideration of the Justice for All Act, has gathered a substantial amount of evidence showing that the Federal court habeas review, particularly in the death penalty area, has suffered from extraordinary delays, some I am told as long as 15 years, for a pending habeas petition to be resolved by a single Federal judge, a misguided application to precedent to frustrate the ends of justice in some instances.

I look forward to hearing from today's witnesses, and I am now pleased to recognize my friend, the distinguished gentleman from Virginia, the Ranking Member of the Subcommittee, Mr. Bobby Scott.

Mr. SCOTT. Thank you, Mr. Chairman. I am pleased to join you in convening this hearing. I would want to make one comment, though, on the death penalty. When you suggest that no innocent people have been executed, it is a fact that some people have been executed, and there has been evidence that could show whether we executed the right man or not. And in some States they will destroy the evidence, in others they will refuse to release the evidence, so you can't find whether they were correct or not. And furthermore, there are a lot of cases where people have been put on death row, and but for DNA evidence they would have been executed. DNA evidence not only in some cases confirmed innocence, but also pointed to the actual perpetrator.

Mr. COBLE. Would the gentleman suspend a moment?

Mr. SCOTT. Yes.

Mr. COBLE. Now, are you talking, Mr. Scott, from 1976 or prior to 1976? I was going post 1976.

Mr. SCOTT. People have been released from death row since 1976, yes, because they have been found innocent through DNA evidence; fair trial, everything else, just had the wrong man. And DNA evidence revealed, exposed the fact that not only did they not do it but also pointed out the one that did.

Now, there is no reason to suspect that people for whom there is no DNA evidence are innocent at any smaller percentage than those for which you lucked out and do have DNA evidence. And so those who have suggested no innocent person has not been executed I think cannot make that case credibly.

But I must say, though, Mr. Chairman, that this hearing has somewhat evolved from what it started with. It started with a hearing where a main focus would be whether or not there was any deterrence value on the death penalty. It has changed to one in which I found the primary issue to be whether the writ of habeas corpus should be essentially eviscerated through H.R. 3035, the so-called Streamlined Procedures Act.

Because of the devastating implications of this bill, and because I am restricted to calling only one witness for this hearing who only has 5 minutes to make his case, the entire focus of our witness had to be devoted to this issue, the habeas corpus issue. This means that the deterrence issue and H.R. 3060, the Terrorist Death Penalty Act, could not be addressed. And that is unfortunate because there is valuable information that needs to be on the record regarding both of these issues, and therefore I feel that we need a separate hearing on this issue. And I want to thank you, Mr. Chairman, for committing to having that separate hearing.

From the initial discussions of our counsels on the hearing, I fully expect that the future witnesses will be those who will be researching the deterrence issue. And I expect one of those—I expected one of those witnesses to be Joanna Shepard or one of her colleagues who would be an economist. She has since qualified her original finding that the death penalty reduced crime following a tirade of criticism and challenges from social scientists and criminal justice researchers. She had stated that executions have an overall deterrent value on the national level, but critics pointed out that her analysis was failed. She has subsequently concluded, as I understand it, that of the 27 States that have had at least one execution during their study period, capital punishment deterred murder in 6 of those States. However, the study suggested that it increased murder in 13 States, or twice as many; in 8 States it had apparently no effect. So on 22 percent of the States executions had a deterrent effect. In contrast, almost 80 percent of the States had either no effect or it actually increased crime.

She concluded that her previously established, quote, deterrent effect had come from 6 States with high execution rates. And if you are going to draw that conclusion, unless you go to those high execution rates in a handful of States, you are better off with no death penalty at all.

H.R. 3035 represents a radical restructuring of traditional applications of the habeas corpus, one of the founding principles of our country. We will hear some issues and problems presented by this bill from our witness, Professor Harcourt, but we really need to focus more attention on the implications of this bill before proceeding further on it.

And so, Mr. Chairman, I look forward to the testimony of our witnesses today and look forward to working with you in our next hearing.

Mr. COBLE. I thank you, Mr. Scott.

We have been joined by the distinguished gentleman from Michigan, the Ranking Member of the full Committee Mr. Conyers, and the distinguished gentleman from Florida and Ohio, respectively, Mr. Feeney and Mr. Chabot, and the gentleman from California, Mr. Lungren.

It is customary to reserve opening statements to Mr. Scott and to me, but when the Ranking Member of the full Committee attends our hearing, I am pleased to recognize him for an opening statement if he has one. Mr. Conyers.

Mr. CONYERS. Thank you, Chairman Coble. I come here to wish that these two bills had been the subject of separate hearings because they are both complex and both very important.

Mr. COBLE. Would the gentleman suspend?

Mr. CONYERS. With pleasure.

Mr. COBLE. Mr. Conyers, before you came—and you may know this—we have also agreed to have a second hearing on these issues as well.

Mr. CONYERS. Yes, thank you. I am happy to know that.

We are dealing with the death penalty, and I have heard the Ranking Subcommittee Member make some important points about it, with which I associate myself, but in the end, the inherent problems with the death penalty is that it sometimes has a reverse deterrent effect and may in fact create martyrs, especially when terrorist-type cases—the Timothy McVeigh situation. There are now over a hundred Americans that have been sentenced to death, only later to be exonerated, which suggests that many of the people convicted and sentenced to death may actually be innocent.

And then in terms of the habeas corpus and stripping Federal courts of their jurisdiction is a very serious matter. Single-handedly, this measure would virtually eliminate the ability of the Federal courts to determine Federal constitutional issues in cases involving prisoners either facing death sentences or serving prison terms. And let's see, the Supreme Court decisions—one, two, three at least—would be overturned, and I think additionally would undermine the overall independence of the Federal judiciary.

I think these matters, both the proposals, contain bad policy, and I look forward to the hearings and ask unanimous consent to insert my statement into the record.

Mr. COBLE. Without objection, the statement will be inserted into the record.

[The prepared statement of Mr. Conyers follows:]

PREPARED STATEMENT OF THE HONORABLE JOHN CONYERS, JR., A REPRESENTATIVE IN CONGRESS FROM THE STATE OF MICHIGAN, AND RANKING MEMBER, COMMITTEE ON THE JUDICIARY

H.R. 3060 offers a solution for a problem and culture that is obviously sorely misunderstood. While it pretends to make us safer, in reality it undermines the solid bit of information that we do know.

For example, we know—thanks to the testimony of the majority's own witness last Congress—that there is no scientific evidence indicating that terrorists will actually be deterred by the threat of capital punishment.

We also know, that with the addition of each new death penalty, we decrease the likelihood of international cooperation and assistance in our efforts to bring suspected terrorists to justice.

Finally, we know—as a result of the events surrounding the execution of convicted Oklahoma City bomber Timothy McVeigh that the execution of terrorists could actually have a reverse deterrent effect through the creation of "martyrs."

In the end, the inherent problems with this bill are the same as those found in many other bills involving the death penalty. Namely, that the system is flawed, defendants rarely receive adequate legal representation and that its application is racially discriminatory.

There are now over 100 Americans that have been sentenced to death, only later to be exonerated. Proving that many of the people convicted and sentenced to death are actually innocent.

Turning attention away from H.R. 3060 and to H.R. 3035, the addition of this bill to the scope of today's hearing proves that the real issue confronting us is about far more than reducing crime and preventing terrorism. As H.R. 3035 clearly demonstrates, it's really about undermining the role of habeas corpus and stripping federal courts of their jurisdiction to determine many federal issues.

Singlehandedly, this bill would virtually eliminate the ability of federal courts to determine federal constitutional issues in cases involving prisoners either facing death sentences or serving prison terms. It would overturn a whole series of Supreme Court decisions; including *Rhines v. Webber* (125 S.Ct. 1528)(2005), *Artuz v. Bennett* (531 U.S. 4)(2000), and *Carey v. Saffold* (593 U.S. 927)(2003). And, it would considerably undermine the overall independence of the federal judiciary.

Quite interestingly, proponents of this bill are some of the same Members of Congress who advocated for the expansion of federal jurisdiction in the case of Terri Schiavo. Now, just a few days later they seek to drastically eliminate it for a countless number of individuals presently involved in our criminal justice system.

Bad politics makes for bad policy. These bills are both. I strongly urge my colleagues to oppose these two measures.

Mr. COBLE. Gentlemen, it is the practice of the Subcommittee to swear in all witnesses appearing before us, so if you would please stand and raise your right hands.

[Witnesses sworn.]

Mr. COBLE. Let the record show that each of the witnesses answered in the affirmative. You may be seated.

We have a very distinguished panel, ladies and gentlemen, let me introduce them to you. We have four distinguished witnesses today. Our first witness is Mr. Barry Sabin, Chief of the Counterterrorism Section of the Criminal Division of the Justice Department. Prior to beginning this role Mr. Sabin served as a Federal criminal trial attorney in the United States Attorney's Office in Miami, Florida, where he held a number of supervisory positions, including the Chief of the Criminal Division and chief of the major prosecutions in the violent crime session.

Prior to joining the Justice Department, he was a litigation associate at Stroock & Stroock & Lavan. Mr. Sabin received his Bachelor's and Master's Degrees from the University of Pennsylvania and his law degree from the New York University School of Law.

Our second witness is the honorable Joshua Marquis, District Attorney General for Clatsop County in Astoria, Oregon. If you will permit me a point of personal privilege, Mr. Marquis, back in the dark ages I served with the Coast Guard at the mouth of the Columbia River, which is your town, and I very much enjoyed being there where it rained just about every day, but I still enjoyed my time on the Columbia River.

Mr. Marquis has been a district attorney since 1994 and has been elected three times since then. He has worked as a prosecutor and defense attorney in Oregon for 20 years. He is past President of the Oregon District Attorney Association and a member of the board of directors of the National District Attorneys Association, where he is chair of that group's Capital Litigation Committee. Mr. Marquis received his undergraduate and law degrees from the University of Oregon.

Our third witness today is Mr. Ronald Eisenberg, the Deputy District Attorney in the Philadelphia District Attorney's Office. Mr. Eisenberg supervises the Law Division, which consists of 60 attorneys. From 1986 through 1991 he was chief of the Appeals Unit in Philadelphia. Previously Mr. Eisenberg served on the Task Force on Death Penalty Litigation of the Third Circuit Court of Appeals and has helped to draft Federal legislative proposals concerning habeas corpus reform and DNA testing. He was awarded his Bachelor's Degree from Haverford College and earned his JD at the University of Pennsylvania School of Law.

Our final witness today is Mr. Bernard Harcourt, Professor of Law and Faculty Director of Academic Affairs at the University of Chicago. Professor Harcourt's scholarship focuses on crime and punishment, and he is the author of "Language of the Gun: Youth, Crime and Public Policy." Previously he practiced law at the Equal Justice Initiative from 1990 to 1994, where he represented death row inmates.

Following law school, he clerked for the honorable Charles Haight, Jr. of the U.S. District Court for the Southern District of New York. Professor Harcourt received his undergraduate degree from Princeton and his JD and PhD Degrees from Harvard.

We have now been joined by the distinguished gentleman from Massachusetts, Mr. Delahunt. Good to have you with us. And I apologize to those in the audience for my lengthy introduction, but I think it benefits all of us to know the outstanding backgrounds and resumes of these gentlemen who will be testifying this afternoon. And the distinguished gentleman from Wisconsin, Mr. Green, has joined us as well.

Gentlemen, as you all have been previously informed, we operate under the 5-minute rule here. The panel that appears before you, the green light is safe waters for you. That green light will turn to amber. And when the red light appears, that is your warning that 5 minutes have expired and Mr. Scott and I may come down after you. I say that figuratively speaking, of course. But if you could confine your remarks to the 5 minutes. We impose the 5-minute rule against ourselves as well, so if you could keep your responses to our questions as terse as possible. Your testimony has been reviewed and will be re-reviewed.

Mr. Sabin, we are happy to recognize you to lead off.

TESTIMONY OF BARRY M. SABIN, CHIEF OF COUNTERTERRORISM SECTION FOR THE CRIMINAL DIVISION, U.S. DEPARTMENT OF JUSTICE

Mr. SABIN. Thank you, Mr. Chairman.

Mr. Chairman, Ranking Member Scott, Members of the Committee, thank you for the opportunity to testify at this important hearing.

I am provided the opportunity to discuss with you the Department of Justice's views on this legislative effort to strengthen penalties for the commission of grave offenses committed by terrorists against the American people and our interests.

The Department of Justice has been committed to the investigation of violent crimes carried out by terrorists against Americans, both within our borders and overseas, for more than a generation. This commitment to the investigation of terrorist attacks has resulted in a considerable number of prosecutions of those who are responsible for bombings, kidnappings, murders and assaults against Americans overseas since the 1980's, as the Department has attempted to use all available legal tools in the fight against terrorism.

As the fight continues, prosecutors must be equipped with every possible legal weapon to help to prevent and deter terrorist conduct before it results in violent action, to severely punish such conduct when it does occur, and to help victims of terrorist crimes by seeking justice on their behalf.

Title I of the Terrorist Death Penalty Enhancement Act of 2005 enhances the existing legal arsenal to ensure that those responsible for the most serious criminal conduct against Americans, conduct that results in death or creates a grave risk of death, will be punished commensurate with the gravity of that crime.

Let me take this opportunity in my oral statement to focus generally on section 103 of the bill, death penalty procedures for certain air piracy cases. My written statement addresses other provisions of the bill under consideration, particularly title III. There are also several other significant changes to the Federal capital punishment statutes that should be considered. The Department stands ready to work with the Committee on these matters.

The Department supports section 103 of the bill, which would permit the imposition of the death penalty upon an individual convicted of air piracy offenses resulting in death where those offenses occurred after enactment of the Antihijacking Act of 1974, but before the enactment of the Federal Death Penalty Act of 1994. This provision would cover a small, but important category of defendants, including those responsible for the December 1984 hijacking of Kuwait Airways Flight 221 and the murder of two American United States Agency for International Development employees, the June 1985 hijacking of TWA Flight 847 and the murder of a Navy diver, the November 1985 hijacking of Egypt Air Flight 648 and the murder of an American servicewoman as well as 56 other passengers, and the September 1986 hijacking of Pan Am Flight 73 and the murder of American citizens Rajesh Kumar and Surendra Patel as well as at least 19 other passengers and crew and the injury of over one hundred others.

Section 103 is important to reaffirm the intent of Congress to have available the ultimate penalty to use against aircraft hijackers whose criminal actions result in death. In 1974, Congress enacted the Antihijacking Act in response to *Furman v. Georgia* to ensure that comprehensive procedures were available so that the death penalty could be constitutionally enforced. Over the years, the crime of air piracy was repeatedly cited by Members of Congress and the executive branch as an example of crime for which Congress has enacted the necessary constitutional provisions to enforce the death penalty.

In 1994, in an effort to make the death penalty widely available for numerous Federal offenses and to enact uniform procedures to apply to all Federal capital offenses, Congress passed the Federal Death Penalty Act of 1994, explicitly including air piracy procedures among the list to which it applies, at the same time repealing the former death penalty procedures of the Antihijacking Act of 1974. The problem with this legal development is that there is a perceived gap in legislative intent to maintain the option of a death penalty for those who committed air piracy resulting in death before enactment of the FDPA.

Let me briefly discuss the circumstances that brought this issue to light. On September 29 of 2001, the United States obtained custody of Zaid Hassan Abd Latif Safarini, the operational leader of the deadly attempted hijacking of Pan Am Flight 73, a crime which occurred on September 5, 1986 in Karachi, Pakistan. Safarini personally executed the first United States citizen, and after a 16-hour standoff he and his fellow hijackers opened fire on approximately 380 passengers and crew on board Pan Am 73, attempting to kill all of them with grenades and assault rifles. In 1991 Safariniand his co-defendants were indicted by a grand jury in the District of Columbia, and after being brought to the United States for trial in 2001, the prosecutors filed papers stating the Government's intention to seek the death penalty against Safarini. The district court, however, ruled that the Government could not seek the death penalty in this case or by implication in any other air piracy case from the pre-FDPA period, essentially because Congress had not made clear which procedures should apply to such prosecution. In its ruling, the court noted that at the time it passed FDPA in 1994 Congress does not state any intention as to whether the new capital sentencing procedures should be applied to air piracy offenses occurring before enactment of the FDPA——

Mr. COBLE. If you would rap up pretty soon, Mr. Sabin.

Mr. SABIN. Section 103 of this bill addresses the issues identified by the district court in the Safarini case by explicitly stating that Congress intends for the provisions of the FDPA to apply to this category of defendants, while also explicitly preserving for such defendants the two provisions of the Antihijacking Act.

I thank the Committee again for holding this hearing and considering this legislation. The Department very much wants to work with Congress to ensure that those who commit serious terrorist crimes are punished to the fullest extent under the law no matter how long it takes to see that justice is done.

[The prepared statement of Mr. Sabin follows:]

PREPARED STATEMENT OF BARRY M. SABIN

Testimony
of
Barry M. Sabin
Chief
Counterterrorism Section
Criminal Division
Department of Justice

Concerning
The Terrorist Death Penalty Enhancement Act of 2005

before the
Subcommittee on Crime, Terrorism and Homeland Security
Committee on the Judiciary
House of Representatives

June 30, 2005

Mr. Chairman, members of the Committee, thank you for the opportunity to testify at this important hearing. I am provided the opportunity to discuss with you the Department of Justice's views on this legislative effort to strengthen penalties for the commission of grave offenses committed by terrorists against the American people and our interests.

I. Introduction

The Department of Justice has been committed to the investigation of violent crimes carried out by terrorists against Americans, both within our borders and overseas, for more than a generation. This commitment to the investigation of terrorist attacks has resulted in a considerable number of prosecutions of those who are responsible for bombings, kidnapings, murders and assaults against Americans overseas since the 1980's, as the Department has attempted to use all available legal tools in the fight against terrorism. As the fight continues, prosecutors must be equipped with every possible legal weapon to help to prevent and deter terrorist conduct before it results in violent action; to severely punish such conduct when it does occur; and to help victims of terrorist crimes by seeking justice on their behalf. Title One of the Terrorist Death Penalty Enhancement Act of 2005 enhances the existing legal arsenal to ensure that those responsible for the most serious criminal conduct against Americans, conduct that results in death or creates a grave risk of death, will be punished commensurate with the gravity of that crime.

I would like to take this opportunity to comment on several particular provisions of the bill under consideration by the Committee.

II. Death Penalty Procedures for Certain Air Piracy Cases

The Department strongly supports Section 103 of the bill, which would permit the imposition of the death penalty upon an individual convicted of air piracy offenses resulting in death where those offenses occurred after enactment of the Antihijacking Act of 1974 but before the enactment of the Federal Death Penalty Act of 1994. This provision would cover a small, but important category of defendants, including those responsible for the December 1984 hijacking of Kuwait Airways flight 221 and the murder of two American United States Agency for International Development employees, William Stanford and Charles Hegna; the June 1985 hijacking of TWA flight 847 and the murder of Navy diver Robert Stethem; the November 1985 hijacking of Egyptair flight 648 and the murder of American servicewoman Scarlett Rogenkamp as well as 56 other passengers; and the September 1986 hijacking of Pan Am flight 73 and the murder of American citizens Rajesh Kumar and Surendra Patel, as well as at least 19 other passengers and crew.

Section 103 is important to reaffirm the intent of Congress to have available the ultimate penalty to use against aircraft hijackers whose criminal actions result in death. In 1974, Congress enacted the Antihijacking Act, making the crime of air piracy the one and only crime under federal law for which Congress passed comprehensive procedures, in response to Furman v. Georgia, 408 U.S. 238 (1972), to ensure that the death penalty could be constitutionally enforced. Over the years after the passage of the Antihijacking Act of 1974, the crime of air piracy was repeatedly cited by members of Congress and the Executive Branch as an example of a crime for which Congress had enacted the necessary constitutional provisions to enforce the death penalty. In 1994, in an effort to make the death penalty widely available for numerous federal offenses, and to enact uniform procedures to apply to all federal capital offenses, Congress passed the Federal Death Penalty Act of 1994 ("FDPA"), explicitly including air piracy procedures among the list of crimes to which it applied, at the same time repealing the former death penalty procedures of the Antihijacking Act of 1974.

The problem with this legal development is that there is a perceived gap in legislative intent to maintain the option of a death penalty for those who committed air piracy resulting in death before enactment of the FDPA. Let me briefly discuss the circumstances that brought this issue to light. On September 29, 2001, the United States obtained custody of Zaid Hassan Abd Latif Safarini, the operational leader of the deadly attempted hijacking of Pan AM flight 73, a crime which occurred on September 5, 1986, in Karachi, Pakistan, and which resulted in the death of at least 20 people, including two United States citizens, and the injury of more than 100 others. Safarini personally executed the first United States citizen and after a 16-hour stand-off, he and his fellow hijackers opened fire on approximately 380 passengers and crew on board Pan Am 73, attempting to kill all of them with grenades and assault rifles. Safarini and his co-defendants had been indicted by a grand jury in the District of Columbia in 1991, and after his capture in 2001, the prosecutors filed papers stating the government's intention to seek the death penalty against Safarini. The district court, however, ruled that the government could not seek the death penalty in this case or, by implication, in any other air piracy case from the pre-FDPA period, essentially because Congress had not made clear which procedures should apply to such a prosecution. In its ruling, the court noted that, at the time it passed the FDPA in 1994, Congress did not state any intention as to whether the new capital sentencing procedures should be applied to air piracy offenses occurring before enactment of the FDPA. A further complication exists, in that there are two provisions of the Antihijacking Act of 1974 which, if taken away from pre-FDPA air piracy defendants, could pose *ex post facto* concerns in light of Ring v. Arizona, 536 U.S. 584 (2002). Safarini has since pled guilty to the charged offenses and was sentenced, pursuant to a plea agreement, to three life terms plus twenty-five years imprisonment.

Section 103 of this bill addresses the issues identified by the district court in the Safarini case by explicitly stating that Congress intends for the provisions of the FDPA to apply to this category of defendants, while also explicitly preserving for such defendants the two provisions of the Antihijacking Act to which they are arguably constitutionally entitled, concerning the statutory aggravating and mitigating circumstances set forth in the Antihijacking Act.

This provision is particularly important for several other reasons. In the absence of a death penalty that could be implemented for pre-FDPA hijacking offenses resulting in death that also occurred before the effective date of the Sentencing Guidelines on November 1, 1987, the maximum penalty available would be life imprisonment. Under the pre-Sentencing Guidelines structure, even prisoners sentenced to life imprisonment were eligible for a parole hearing after serving only ten years. While there is a split in the Circuit Courts of Appeals as to whether a sentencing judge can impose a sentence that could avert the 10-year parole hearing requirement, the current position of the Bureau of Prisons is that a prisoner is eligible for a parole hearing after serving ten years of a life sentence. Even if parole is denied on that first occasion, such prisoners are entitled to have regularly scheduled parole hearings every two years thereafter. Moreover, in addition to parole eligibility after ten years, the old sentencing and parole laws incorporated a presumption that even persons sentenced to life imprisonment would be released after no more than 30 years.

In the context of the individuals responsible for the hijacking incidents described above, most of the perpetrators were no older than in their 20's when they committed their crimes. The imposition of a pre-Guidelines sentence of life imprisonment for these defendants means that many, if not all of them, could be expected to be released from prison well within their lifetime. Given the gravity of these offenses, coupled with the longstanding Congressional intent to have a death penalty available for the offense of air piracy resulting in death, such a result would be at odds with the clear directive of Congress.

Section 103 of the bill, as proposed, does not, however, include a very important component, a severability clause. The Department strongly recommends adding in a severability clause that would establish that if any provision of the Act or the application thereof to any person or circumstance is held invalid by a court of law, the remainder of Section 103 and the application of such provision to other persons or circumstances shall not be affected by that declaration of invalidity. By including a severability clause such as the one recommended, the unaffected portions of the law would remain operable.

III. Modification of Federal Death Penalty Procedures

Title III of the bill addresses a number of concerns regarding the current federal capital punishment statutory scheme. The Department generally supports these proposals and believes that, for the most part, they would improve upon existing law. These proposals are a good start to addressing certain issues of concern. There are, however, several other, more significant changes to the federal capital punishment statutes that can and should be considered. The Department stands ready to discuss additional changes with the Committee.

The bill's proposal in Section 301(a) to eliminate Title 21 death penalty provisions in favor of application of the Title 18 death penalty provisions has been contemplated for years. This measure is advisable to ensure uniformity of application of procedures in capital cases and eliminate confusion engendered by two overlapping procedures. (The Title 18 procedures purport to be applicable to all capital offenses.) It should be noted that subsection (q) of the Title 21 procedures applies not only to federal capital prosecutions, but also to the appointment of qualified counsel and experts in federal *habeas corpus* review of state capital convictions. Thus, the subsection should not be eliminated in its entirety without consideration of the consequences.

The proposal in Section 301(b) to modify the death penalty mitigating factor relating to equally culpable defendants would eliminate the ability of defendants to rely on the statutory mitigating factor if the government sought but did not obtain a death sentence for a co-defendant. The Department favors this amendment. The Department believes that a sentence received by a co-defendant is not mitigating evidence that the Constitution requires a jury to be allowed to consider. Mitigating evidence within the constitutional construct is limited to aspects of the defendant's character, background or circumstances of the offense. The Department believes that the sentence received by a co-defendant does not fit within any of these categories of mitigating evidence and does not reflect on the culpability of the defendant. It must be recognized, however, that courts may nonetheless admit such evidence as a non-statutory mitigating factor.

The Department has no objection to Section 301(c), which adds several situations to those that can be considered as aggravating factors. It creates an "obstruction of justice" aggravating factor. It expands aggravating factors to include whether a defendant created the expectation of payment of anything of pecuniary value in the procurement of the commission of the capital offense. It also adds to the list of offenses that constitute aggravating factors in 18 U.S.C. § 3592(c)(1) the various crimes identified in 18 U.S.C. § 2339E.

Section 301(d) would allow for empaneling a new jury if an existing jury deadlocks on sentencing. If enacted, this provision would represent a major change in federal capital punishment practice and procedure. The provision would appear to respond to the Supreme

Court's decision in Jones v. United States, 527 U.S. 373, 379-81 (1999). Arguably, however, the new provision could be seen as conflicting with 18 U.S.C. § 3594, as interpreted by the Supreme Court, and therefore, the Department recommends that § 3594 also be reviewed to foreclose this conflict. Consideration should also be given to whether Section 301(d) would limit the prosecution on retrial of punishment to those aggravating factors that were found by the previous jury beyond a reasonable doubt. If this is the case, thought needs to be given to incorporating this limitation into the statute.

The Department also supports proposed Section 301(e), which would authorize the trial court to proceed with a death penalty case with fewer than 12 jurors if the court finds "good cause" for this action or, as is the case under current law, the parties stipulate to a smaller number with the approval of the court. There are a variety of circumstances that could bring this provision into play, including the loss of jurors over the course of a lengthy trial. In one instance, the trial court excused the alternate jurors at the conclusion of the guilt phase of the trial. In that case, if one additional juror had been lost during the punishment hearing, the prosecution would have been unable to proceed without the concurrence of the defense. There is little incentive for a defendant to stipulate to a punishment hearing before fewer than 12 jurors.

The Department supports Section 301(g), which proposes to increase the number of alternate jurors from a maximum of six to a maximum of nine persons, and to increase the number of available peremptory challenges from three to four due to the additional alternate jurors. The Department believes that this proposal is desirable, because a capital sentencing hearing significantly lengthens the duration of a trial, and may significantly increase the potential loss of jurors during such a trial. If adopted, this provision should be added to Rule 24 of the Federal Rules of Criminal Procedure as subparagraph (c)(4)(D), to follow the existing subparagraph (c)(4)(C), which should not be impliedly repealed by the amendment.

IV. Conclusion

I thank the Committee again for holding this hearing and considering this legislation. The Department very much wants to work with Congress to ensure that those who commit serious terrorist crimes are punished to the fullest extent of the law, no matter how long it takes to see that justice is done.

I will do my best to answer your questions.

Mr. COBLE. The gentleman's time has expired.
Mr. Marquis.

TESTIMONY OF THE HONORABLE JOSHUA K. MARQUIS, DISTRICT ATTORNEY, CLATSOP COUNTY, OREGON

Mr. MARQUIS. Thank you, Mr. Chairman. Thank you for inviting me here today.

As you have indicated, I am from Astoria, the classic county. It is where Lewis and Clark ended their trail 200 years ago. And my wife's family is from your State, and she constantly complains about the rain all the time, so—but you are all welcome to come.

I have been a trial lawyer for 20 years, and I've had the unusual experience of having served as lead counsel as both a prosecutor and as a defense attorney in capital cases. I have co-authored a book on the death penalty, and I debate this subject around the United States and Europe. And with all due respect to the Chair, I am a lifelong Democrat. I have never voted for a Republican for President, and probably won't.

Mr. COBLE. Mr. Marquis, as Mr. Scott will tell you, he and I get along—and Mr. Delahunt as well, and Mr. Conyers. We all get along pretty well, despite their shortcomings.

Mr. DELAHUNT. No apologies here.

Mr. MARQUIS. Well, I mention that only to make clear that I think this discussion transcends traditional liberal conservative or Republican-Democrat issues. There needs to be something very vigorous in a discussion as serious as the death penalty, and when we're talking about the State taking lives, even particularly those of terrorists. And there are people of good will on both sides of this issue, but it is very critical that we have an honest debate and, as Mr. Scott says, I am here to talk today about deterrence primarily.

In my written statement I detail what I consider a series of urban legends that exist about the death penalty in the United States. Basically the death penalty is crowded with innocent men—mostly men, there's a few women. Nothing could be further from the truth. The capital justice system in the United States, like all other parts of the system, is not without its faults. There is no human endeavor that is not.

A death sentence is handed down in the United States, since 1976, in approximately one out of every thousand murders. So we are talking about a very rare occasion—and it should be a rare occasion. Even Judge Jed Rakoff of the U.S. District Court of New York, who ruled the death penalty unconstitutional because he claims so many innocent people might be executed, has conceded that the number is about 30 of the 8,000 people sentenced to death since Gregg in 1976. That would be the error rate at about, I think, one-third of 1 percent. And frankly, you have a better chance of being killed by your pharmacist or elective surgery than you do of a faulty death penalty. And as the Chairman mentioned, the number of people who have been found innocent, who have later found out to be executed—and there were those before

1976—that number since 1976 is zero, despite very hard work by a lot of death penalty opponents to try to prove that.

Now even more compelling, I think, in the context of this hearing, is what will happen if we fail to condemn the worst of the worst in our society. There is a study just out by a very noted liberal or progressive professor from the University of Chicago—I believe, in fact, he is a colleague of Professor Harcourt—named Cass Sunstein, who has just published a very provocative paper called, "Is Capital Punishment Morally Required?" and he cites an increasing cluster of studies which show a clear deterrent effect between the death penalty and reductions in murders, and asks, what will we say to the families of murder victims when we could have prevented those people's deaths? And he makes the point more eloquently than I can that we have about 50 executions a day in the United States, and they are conducted very capriciously and they are not conducted by the Government.

Unfortunately, we do know the names of people, innocent people killed as a result of our failure to have the death penalty. Ask the families of Kenneth McDuff's victims from Texas on death row; out again, killed seven people. Or I am sure Attorney General Lungren remembers Robert Massey in California, on death row, released; he rewards the man who gives him a job by killing him. He was eventually put to death.

In my written testimony, I detail a popular movie and play called "The Exonerated," which claims to chronicle the story of six people on death row who are now off death row who they claim to be innocent. The problem is that two of those two people pled guilty, and the third one is not available to do press tours right now because he's doing time in New York for a murder he pled guilty to, which is identical to the one for which he was acquitted, and for that reason he was exonerated.

There is a very good reason that the opponents of the death penalty use words like "exonerated" and "innocent." they are very powerful words, they mean something very significant, and I think to use that word when it is not appropriate dishonors the names of the people who really were innocent. And Mr. Scott will point out there have been people who have been on death row who have been innocent, and that is something we need to work very hard against.

I see that I have very little time remaining. I want to briefly touch on the issue of race because I think it is very important.

There is also a very common belief the death penalty is inherently racist. And I recommend a study, again by a group of academics who are against the death penalty, from Cornell University last year who showed that the traditional theories that the so-called South is a death belt is simply not true. In fact, States of the Confederacy tend to fall below the average. Oregon, my State, is just above, and Texas is just below. The States with the highest rates of death penalty are Ohio and Delaware and Nevada.

The larger issue is how we can achieve a flawless system, and I don't think we're going to be able to do that. Support for the death penalty does not mean that you enthusiastically support capital punishment. And again, the fear of offending perhaps the pro-life members, I am pro-choice, I amfor the death penalty in the same way I am for abortion; I would rather not see abortions and I would rather not see capital punishment but I think it is something that is a necessity.

Thank you very much for inviting me today.

[The prepared statement of Mr. Marquis follows:]

PREPARED STATEMENT OF JOSHUA K. MARQUIS

TESTIMONY OF HON. JOSHUA K. MARQUIS
DISTRICT ATTORNEY - CLATSOP COUNTY, OREGON

BEFORE THE
UNITED STATES HOUSE OF REPRESENTATIVES
JUDICIARY COMMITTEE
SUBCOMITTEE ON CRIME AND TERRORISM

JUNE 30, 2005

For decades in America questions about the death penalty centered on philosophical and sometimes religious debate over the morality of the state-sanctioned execution of another human being. Public opinion ebbed and flowed with support for the death penalty declining as civil rights abuses became a national concern in the 1960s and increasing along with a rapid rise in violent crime in the 1980s.

Those who oppose capital punishment call themselves "abolitionists," clearly relishing the comparison to those who fought slavery in the 19th century. In the mid 1990s these abolitionists, funded by a cadre of wealthy supporters including George Soros and Roderick MacArthur, succeeded in changing the focus of the debate over the death penalty from the morality of executions to questions about the "fundamental fairness" or, in their minds, unfairness of the institution. The abolitionists were frustrated by polling that showed that virtually all groups of Americans supported capital punishment in some form in some cases.

Led by Richard Dieter of the neutral-sounding "Death Penalty Information Center," opponents of capital punishment undertook a sweeping make-over of their campaign. In addition to painting America as a rogue state, a wolf among the peaceful lambs of the European Union who had forsaken the death penalty, the latter-day abolitionists sought to convince America that as carried out the death penalty was inherently racist, that the unfortunates on death row received wretched and often incompetent defense counsel, and, most appalling, that a remarkable number of those sentenced to death were in fact innocent.

Dieter and his allies pointed to the fact that while African-Americans make up only slightly more than 10 percent of the American population, they constitute more than 40 percent of those on death row. They described cases in which the lawyers appointed to represent someone facing execution were in some cases nothing more than golfing pals with the judge making the appointment, that some of these lawyers had no previous experience with murder cases, and that in at least one case the lawyer appears to have slept through portions of the trial.

Abolitionists painted a picture of massive prosecution, funded by the endless resources of the government pitted against threadbare public defenders either barely out of law school or, if experienced, pulled from the rubbish heap of the legal profession.

But most compelling of all the arguments that called capital punishment "fatally flawed" were the stories of men who had served years on death row, a few coming close to their scheduled execution only to be released because a court had determined that they were "exonerated." Television programs showed dramatic footage of Anthony Porter, freed from Illinois' death row, running into the arms of his savior, Northwestern University journalism professor David Protess. A handful of other stories of "innocents on death row" filled magazines, television programs, and symposia on college campuses across the country.

In the face of horrific crimes like the murder of more than 160 people by Timothy McVeigh, death penalty opponents sought to recruit new converts. By the time of the 2000 presidential campaign they had succeeded in moving the debate to a point where supporters of capital punishment felt beleaguered and outgunned. A growing number of classic conservatives, from William F. Buckley to Pat Robertson, expressed their mistrust of capital punishment. The arguments succeeded in driving down public support for the death penalty from a high of over 80 percent in the 1980s to a low of 63 percent in the year George W. Bush ran against Al Gore for president.

Recognizing the polls still showed majority support for the existence of the death penalty, abolitionists started advocating for a "moratorium," suggesting that short of abolition, a halt should be declared to executions while the issue was intensively studied. They found an unlikely ally in then-Governor George Ryan of Illinois.

Ryan, a conservative Republican, had just two years earlier, in 1998, won election in part by underlining his support for capital punishment. But in 1999 the Chicago *Tribune* began running a hard-hitting series of lengthy articles accusing Illinois prosecutors of serious misconduct and highlighting a number of cases in which men sentenced to death row had been released when appellate courts found serious errors in their trials or claims of misconduct by police or prosecutors. Although prosecutors and at least one state supreme court justice questioned Ryan's authority simply to halt the death penalty process, Ryan's action effectively prevented the execution of any of the 170 men on that state's death row.

Ryan became a folk hero. He was lauded on college campuses across the country, cited as a profile in political courage by foreign politicians, and was even nominated for the Nobel Peace prize. Just before leaving office in 2003 Ryan stunned many when he announced a sweeping clemency, using his executive powers to release 167 men from death row and granting outright pardons to four more.

Sensing a possible sea change in public sentiment, the abolitionists pushed for other states to follow Ryan's example. The moratorium became the leading campaign issue in the Maryland governor's race in 2002.

After these apparent victories, the tide did start to turn, but not the way the abolitionists expected.

Governor Ryan was dogged by a federal investigation into bribery and corruption charges that drove his approval rating to less than 25 percent. His name became so toxic in Illinois politics that the Republican candidate, whose last name was also Ryan but was no relation to the Governor, campaigned on first name. After securing indictments and convictions against his top aides and even his campaign committee, federal prosecutors indicted Ryan on charges of bribery, corruption, and racketeering.

In Maryland, Democratic gubernatorial candidate Kathleen Kennedy Townsend's pledge to seek a death penalty moratorium was cited as a prime reason for her defeat in that election.

The murder of 3,000 people [they weren't all either Americans or New Yorkers] on September 11, 2001 reminded many Americans that some crimes merited the ultimate punishment.

Having largely abandoned the moral arguments against capital punishment, the modern abolition movement is now based on a trio of urban legends:
The death penalty is racist at its core;
Those accused of capital murder get grossly inadequate representation;
A remarkable number of people on death row are innocent.

* * * * *

In the last ten years the violent crime rate in America, including the murder rate, has decreased dramatically. A series of studies[1] by economists in 2001 showed an undeniable correlation between the death penalty and deterrence.

One researcher who reported that pardons may have actually costs lives nonetheless added a postscript to the study, saying that despite the results of his study he personally believed that the death penalty remained biased against minorities.

How could the death penalty not be racially biased given the disproportionate number of African-Americans on death row? A Cornell University study issued in March of 2004 by

---

[1] Dezhbakhsh, Rubin & Sheperd, "Deterrence and the Death Penalty," Emory University, 2001. Dale O. Cloninger and Roberto Marchesini., "Execution Moratorium Is No Holiday For Homicides", *Applied Economics*, Vol 33, No. 5, April, 2001. H. Noci Mocan and R. Kaj Gittings , "Pardons, Executions and Homicide", National Bureau of Economic Research, Working Paper 8639, December 2001.

law professors John Blume and Theodore Eisenberg and statistician Martin Wells – all avowed opponents of the death penalty – showed that the conventional wisdom about the South's so-called "death belt," where blacks are said to be much more likely to die than whites convicted of similar murders, simply doesn't hold up. In the words of the authors, " The conventional wisdom about the death penalty is incorrect in some respects and misleading in others."

Until the Cornell study, for their accusations of racism the abolitionists had relied largely the studies of David Baldus, an Iowa law professor, who claimed that the race of the murderer was the greatest determiner of whether the death penalty would be imposed

The Cornell University study, drawn from statistics gathered by the U.S. Department of Justice's Bureau of Justice Statistics, showed that while African-Americans were convicted of committing 51 percent of all murders , they comprised only 41 percent of death row's population. The study noted that barely 10 of the murders were cross-racial and that in 28 states, including Georgia, South Carolina and Tennessee, blacks were under-represented on death row. States like Texas which had the greatest number of people on death row actually had a lower per capita rate of imposing the death penalty than Nevada, Ohio, and Delaware.

The Cornell study thereby confirmed what many prosecutors had suspected – that a white murderer sentenced to die was twice as likely to actually be executed than a black person convicted of the same crime. It may be shockingly politically incorrect to say, but the fact is that the most horrific murders -- serial killings, torture murders, and sex crimes against children -- tend to be committed more frequently by white murderers than blacks.

The next urban legend is that of the threadbare but plucky public defender fighting against all odds against a team of sleek, heavily-funded prosecutors with limitless resources. The reality in the 21st century is startlingly different. There is no doubt that before the landmark 1963 decision in <u>Gideon vs. Wainwright</u>, appointed counsel was often inadequate. But the past few decades have seen the establishment of public defender systems that in many cases rival some of the best lawyers retained privately. The Chicago *Tribune*, while slamming the abilities of a number of individual defense counsel in capital cases in the 1980s in Cook County, grudgingly admitted that the Cook County Public Defender's Office provided excellent representation for its indigent clients.

Many giant silk-stocking law firms in large cities across America not only provide pro-bono counsel in capital cases, they also offer partnerships to lawyers whose sole job is to promote indigent capital defense. In one recent case in Alabama, a Portland, Oregon law firm spent hundreds of thousands of dollars of lawyer time on a post-conviction appeal for a death row inmate. In Oregon, where I have both prosecuted and defended capital cases, it is common for attorneys to be paid hundreds of thousands of dollars by the state for their representation of indigent capital clients. And the funding is not limited to legal assistance. Expert witnesses for the defense often total tens of thousands of dollars each, resources far beyond the reach of individual district attorneys who prosecute the same cases.

As the elected prosecutor of what is considered a mid-sized county in Oregon, I have a set budget that rarely gives me more than $15,000 a year the cover the total expenses of expert witnesses for <u>all</u> the hundreds of cases my office prosecutes each year. Yet in one recent murder trial one witness in the mitigation phase admitted he had already billed the state indigent defense program for over $30,000. In a related case the investigators for the defense were paid over $100,000.

Scott Turow, the bestselling novelist, spent some time as a federal prosecutor before joining a high-end Chicago law firm. He became interested in the death penalty through pro bono work he and his firm performed for a group of death row defendants who were eventually released. Governor Ryan appointed Turow to a 17-member commission that sought to review Illinois' death penalty laws. The commission was heavily laden with "former prosecutors" like Turow, who were now criminal defense lawyers. Only one commission member was a sitting prosecutor. That member, Mike Waller, was the lone dissenter on many of the recommendations that were adopted almost in their entirety by the Illinois legislature.

Turow has written two recent books, one fictional -- *Reversible Errors*, already a TV movie-of-the-week -- and a slim, austere volume of his personal reflections, *Ultimate Punishment*. The novel sold well, like most of Turow' s other works. It paints the traditional urban myth of over-zealous and politically-ambitious prosecutors and incompetent forensics resulting in a tragic miscarriage of justice, thwarted by a brave civil attorney who is dabbling in pro-bono capital defense work, aided by his love interest, a recovering addict who sold her office as a judge and fell from grace.

Popular culture, most of it not as well crafted as Turow's, has created an entire alternate universe that nutures a legal system that regularly hurls doe-eyed innocents onto death row through the malevolent machinations of corrupt cops and district attorneys who either earn bonuses for the innocent people they convict or are so intent on advancing their careers that they disregard the truth and conceal evidence that might clear the defendant.

These fantastic constructions are prominent in television programs like *The Practice* (mercifully axed), in movies like *True Believer* and *True Crime,* as well as in popular fiction. There is an axiom in journalism that it's not news how many planes landed safely today. Accordingly, it's not surprising that the news articles that make the front page of major publications are about the exceedingly rare cases where the convicted defendant did not, in fact, commit the offense.

One of the most striking examples of truth and fiction blended in popular culture is a play called "The Exonerated," which just finished a successful two-year run off-Broadway and is now touring the United States. The play profiles six people who were once on death

row and now walk free. The clear implication is that they are innocent in the classic sense of that word – that they didn't do it, weren't there, didn't participate. Yet of the six, two (Sonia "Sunny" Jacobs and Kerry Cook) stand convicted by their own guilty pleas of the murders for which they were supposedly "exonerated."
Neither the script nor the reviews of, nor most of the press for "The Exonerated" bear any resemblance to the stark facts of the case.

"Imagine everything you did between the years of 1976 and 1992. Now remove all of it. Those 16 years were taken away from Sunny Jacobs, convicted and sentenced to death for a crime she did not commit. But her story is not unique, and it could happen just as easily to you. "The Exonerated" tells the true stories of six innocent survivors of death row."

- website for the play "The Exonerated"

Susan Sarandon, Debra Winger, Mia Farrow, Vanessa Redgrave and other stars of stage and screen have been pleased at the chance to read the words of a woman who stands convicted of two murders. Rated the third-best play of 2002 by *Time* magazine, veteran theater critic John Simon declared that "docudramas can take liberties with the truth in subtle, sometimes unintentional ways," but he has "no reason to disbelieve" authors Erik Jensen and Jessica Blank's version of the truth. Obviously Mr. Simon has only seen and read the play, not the trial. In fact, Sunny Jacobs, the main character in "The Exonerated," is both legally and factually guilty, a woman who has been exonerated only by theater critics or other glitterati who take these claims at face value.

The play recently visited Phoenix, Arizona, where one reviewer recounted that "[Jacobs] and her husband were taken hostage by the man who committed the crimes." In an English production of the play Jacobs is described as a "yoga instructor" who calls herself a "hippie. I was a peace and love person. I'm a vegetarian." No mention of her several arrests for gun, drug, and prostitution charges or her admissions that she participated in gunning down two men. Another review calls her "a young mother trying to protect her children and her mate, . . . caught in a police shooting…."

Here are the facts, gained from the trial transcripts, published opinions of the Florida Supreme Court and the 11th US Circuit Court of Appeals, and from reviewing the tapes and transcripts of police interrogations.

Canadian constable Donald Irwin was on a "ride-along" with his friend Phillip Black, a trooper for the Florida State Police, on the morning of February 20, 1976. Trooper Black had met Corporal Irwin of the Ontario Provincial Police and the two had visited each other 's homes over the years.

Black and Irwin were checking a car parked at a rest stop along I-95 near Pompano Beach. The Camaro was occupied by two men -- Jesse Tafero (Jacob's boyfriend and the father of their infant son) and a prison pal of Tafero's named Walter Rhodes -- and Jacobs and her two children. Two truck drivers saw the trooper order the men out of the car, leaving only Jacobs and her two children in the car. After they got out of the car at least one shot was fired from inside. Several more shots were fired, all from guns Jacobs had purchased in North Carolina.

Both Irwin and Black lay dead when the group stole the trooper's car and took off. One witness saw a man later identified as Rhodes with his hands in full view (ie., no gun in hand). A TASER dart was discovered in the door of the cruiser. In the Camaro a discharged TASER gun was found in the back seat near where Jacobs and her kids had been seated. Two expended shells from the semi-automatic pistols registered to Jacobs were found inside as well, consistent with the shots being fired from inside the car.

After taking the trooper's car, the group then kidnapped an elderly man and his Cadillac, initially claiming they had to take a sick child to the hospital. With Rhodes at the wheel and with the 9mm pistol (owned by Jacobs) strapped to a holster around Tafero's waist, they tried to run a roadblock. Police opened fire and shot Rhodes in the leg. The group surrendered.

Officers initially were unclear about Jacobs' relationship to the men. She clarified it by kissing Tafero and later telling her nine-year old that she loved him and for him "to keep his mouth shut." Shortly thereafter Jacobs responded to a comment about how "it felt to shoot a trooper": "We had to," she said, and while being transported she told officers that she had fired the first shot.

Jacobs' version in the play? "It all happened so fast, you know. I just ducked down to cover the kids....We were kidnapped at that point....I know there must be a roadblock. 'Hey we're gonna be rescued. Help is on the way, you know, the cavalry."

The prosecution gave Walter Rhodes, who denied firing any of the fatal shots, a lie detector test; when he passed they allowed him to plead guilty to murder in the second degree. He agreed to testify against Jesse Tafero and Sunny Jacobs. Tafero was tried first, convicted, and sentenced to death. Jacobs was tried next and also convicted. Although gushing reviews of "The Exonerated" refer to "readings from actual transcripts," Jacobs never testified at trial before a jury. Her only testimony was before a judge in a pre-trial motion, seeking to keep statements she made to investigators away from the trial jury. She chose to invoke her constitutional right not to testify, but now wants to be vindicated in the court of public opinion, where there is no 5th Amendment. The jury recommended life in prison but the judge over-ruled the jury and imposed a death sentence.

The Florida Supreme Court in turn over-ruled the trial judge and reduced the sentence to life. Jacobs served two years on death row, not sixteen as the play would have the audience believe, before being released into the prison's general population. Another decade went by and the case ended up before the federal appeals court that oversees Florida. In ordering a new trial, the 11th Circuit also denied Sunny Jacobs' claims of factual innocence but held that a polygraph -- which was inadmissible and which Rhodes passed -- contained answers that were inconsistent with some of Rhodes' testimony. The appeals court ruled that the answers should have been turned over to the defense in the Jacobs trial, and therefore warranted a new trial for Jacobs.

Jacobs was represented by top-notch defense counsel who had become personally devoted to her cause. She was released from prison in 1992 after en tering an "Alford" guilty plea (the defendant is allowed to claim she didn't really commit the crime but is pleading guilty to take advantage of the plea offer) to two counts of Murder 2 (the same charges to which Rhodes pled). At the plea and sentencing hearing the prosecutor recited the facts the state could prove. Jacobs and her lawyers agreed the state could prove those facts. Witnesses had died and Rhodes had recanted and then unrecanted at least twice. After 16 years of battling in the courts, the prosecutor decided that a plea to Murder in the Second Degree and 17 years in prison was an acceptable result.

In the play, the clear impression is that Sunny Jacobs was freed from prison by a guardian angel: "But after all that, one day, a guard came into my cell and told me I was getting out. I thought he was trying to trick me."

No court ever "exonerated" Sonia Jacobs. She was convicted of the same crime as Walter Rhodes (who now claims his original testimony was correct), who actually served more time than Jacobs. She is *legally guilty by virtue of a plea and sentence*. But she came from a wealthy white family. Her background isn't what people expect from a murderer. The elegant Mimi Rogers played her in a made-for-TV movie, *In the Blink of an Eye*, which aired on ABC in 1996. The inconvenient facts of her cold-blooded executions of two innocent men from the back seat of a Camaro while her nine-year-old son looked on were deleted from the movie, to make her release from prison palatable to the television audience.

The urban legend of actual innocence flourishes.

In an article published November 27, 2003, Contra Costa *Times* reporter Georgia Rowe glibly parroted, "American history is rife with people who were convicted of crimes they didn't commit."

In 1998, Northwestern University sponsored a conference that celebrated a group of people it claimed were innocents on death row. One of the men on stage was Dr. Jay Smith, made infamous by Joseph Wambaugh's book *Echoes in the Darkness* and one of the 87 men Amnesty International fetes as having been "freed from death row." The real story is not so festive.

Dr. Smith was convicted of the murder of high school English teacher Susan Reinert and her two children. A jury concluded that Smith and another teacher had conspired to murder Reinert, and that her children were collateral damage of the murder scheme, killed because they might have given witness. Reinert's body was recovered, but the children have never been found.

A state appellate court held that prosecutors had failed to disclose the existence on the victim's body of a few grains of sand that might possibly have supported Smith's claim of innocence. Smith's conviction was set aside and he was freed from a life sentence in prison. Emboldened by his newfound freedom (and despite his undisturbed convictions for theft by deception, receiving stolen property, possession of a firearm without a license and possession of marijuana), Smith filed lawsuits against the State of Pennsylvania, the officer who arrested him and everyone connected with his prosecution.

There was only one problem: Smith was not innocent. In its final decision throwing Smith's case out of court, the U.S. Circuit Court of Appeals for the Third Circuit concluded: "Our confidence in Smith's convictions for the murder of Susan Reinert and her two children is not the least bit diminished by consideration of the suppressed lifters and quartz particles, and Smith has therefore not established that he is entitled to compensation for the unethical conduct of some of those involved in the prosecution."

Yes, there are a few people who actually did not do it. Some are true poster boys: Kirk Bloodsworth, a Maryland man who was convicted of murder and later exonerated by DNA testing. Cases like Bloodsworth show that the years and layers of appeals required in capital cases do in fact catch the rare mistake that wrongfully jails or condemns an innocent man.

Most have stories more akin to Anthony Porter, whose release was due in large part to the work of journalism students at Northwestern University. What doesn't make it into the stock footage of him running jubilantly into the arms of Professor Protess upon his release from prison is how he got to prison in the first place. Porter was committing an armed robbery in the same park, at the same time as a drug murder. He ran from the park, gun in hand, in full view of witnesses who identified Porter to the police. Porter denied not only the murder, but even being in the park, a lie he maintained until after his convictions were affirmed.

The justice system is far from perfect and has made many mistakes, mostly in *favor* of the accused. Hundreds if not thousands have died or lost their livelihoods through embezzlement or rape because the American justice system failed to incarcerate people who were guilty by any definition.

Since the death penalty was re-authorized in 1976 by the Supreme Court, there have been upwards of 500,000 murders. About 7,000 murderers were sentenced to death and about 3,700 remain on death row today. Seven hundred and fifty have been executed. Appellate courts at the state and federal levels have imposed what one justice called "super due process" for convicted capital murderers, overturning almost two-thirds of all death sentences, a rate far exceeding that in other cases. Virtually none have been overturned because of " actual innocence."

Some claim that a civilized society must be prepared to allow ten guilty men to walk free in order to spare one innocent. But the well-organized and even better-funded abolitionists cannot point to a single case of a demonstrably innocent person executed in the modern era of American capital punishment.

Instead, let's tally the *additional* victims of the freed:

Nine, killed by Kenneth McDuff, who had been sentenced to die for child murder in Texas and then was freed on parole after the death penalty laws at the time were overturned.

One, by Robert Massie of California, also sentenced to die and also paroled. Massie rewarded the man who gave him a job on parole by murdering him less than a year after getting out of prison.

One, by Richard Marquette, in Oregon, sentenced to "life" (which until 1994 meant about eight years in Oregon) for abducting and then dismembering women. He did so well in a woman-free environment (prison) that he was released – only to abduct, kill and dismember women again.

Two, by Carl Cletus Bowles, in Idaho, guilty of kidnapping nine people and the murder of a police officer. Bowles escaped during a conjugal visit with a girlfriend, only to abduct and murder an elderly couple.

The victims of these men didn't have "close calls" with death. They are dead. Murdered. Without saying goodbye to their loved ones. Without appeal to the state or the media or Hollywood or anyone's heartstrings.

Discouraged over polls that have consistently shown public support for capital punishment between 65 and 85 percent over the last quarter century, proponents of the death penalty have decided to tap into an understandable horror that people who are truly innocent of the murder of which they stand convicted are on death row. They are turning into doe-eyed innocents the few murderers who have slipped through one of the countless cracks in the law afforded to capital defendants. They want us to believe that any one of us could be snatched at any time from our daily freedoms and sentenced to die because of a false and coerced confession, police corruption, faulty eyewitness identification, botched forensics, prosecutorial misconduct, and shoddy and ill-paid defense counsel.

There are a handful of people who have spent time, in some cases many years, on death row, for crimes they genuinely did not commit. The number bandied about by the abolitionists just passed the 100 mark. But a closer examination using a more realistic definition of innocence –that is, had no involvement in the death, wasn't there, didn't do it – drops the number to 30 or even 25. At a seminar in February of 2004 held by the Federal Bar Council of New York, US District Court Judge Jed Rakoff, who made history in 2001 by ruling the death penalty unconstitutional, acknowledged that his research showed the number to be closer to 30. The larger question is whether the problem of wrongful convictions in capital cases is an episodic or epidemic problem.

For those who believe that no rate of error is acceptable, the death penalty can never be "reformed" sufficiently, despite the claims that they are seeking only to insure a fairer system. Yet these same advocates urge the substitution of life without parole, claiming (as is sometimes true) that many inmates consider a life sentence to be worse than execution. Peel back the layers of this reckoning and you'll find these advocates claiming that it is just as horrible to threaten to take away the remaining da ys of a murderer's life, and therefore we must abolish all long prison sentences as well as the death penalty.

The number of death sentences is, in fact, decreasing. Criminal sentences for crimes other than murder have become tougher, terms of imprisonment more certain, and perhaps more significantly, the rate of murder is down overall. Prosecutors and juries are properly and appropriately becoming even more discriminating about determining who should die for their crimes. It is a journey not taken lightly.

Likewise, casting the accused as true innocents caught up by a corrupt and uncaring system only discredits a movement that has legitimate moral arguments. Nothing excuses making the victims nameless and faceless, making martyrs out of murderers, and turning killers into victims.

(What follows below is a detailed analysis of the Death Penalty Information Center's list of "Exonerated" off death row complied and used with the permission of Ward Campbell, a career Assistant Attorney General in the California Department of Justice)

CRITIQUE OF DPIC LIST ("INNOCENCE: FREED FROM DEATH ROW")

Ward A. Campbell[1], Supervising Assistant Attorney General, State of California

Updated: June 24, 2005

The Death Penalty Information Center (DPIC) Innocence List ("Innocence: Freed from Death Row")[2] [hereinafter the "DPIC List" or "List"] is currently cited as support for the claim that 119 innocent prisoners have been released from Death Rows across the nation.[3] This List is uncritically accepted as definitive. However, an examination of the premises and sources of the List raises serious questions about whether many of the allegedly innocent Death Row prisoners named on the List are actually innocent at all or whether their cases should be cited as evidence of problems with our capital punishment system.

Analysis of the cases on the List suggests that the DPIC exaggerates the number of inaccurate capital convictions. In many instances, the List jumps to conclusions and misstates the implications of what has happened in the various cases that it cites as involving "actually innocent" defendants. The DPIC "falsely exonerates" many of the former Death Row members on its List and misleads the public about the frequency of wrongful convictions in terms of appraising the current capital punishment system in this country.

As of June 24, 2005, the DPIC cites 119 cases of "innocent" defendants released from Death Row–approximately 1.6% of the total number of death sentences imposed between 1973 and 2003.It relies on this number and the cases it represents to claim there is a "crisis in our system of justice." However, it is arguable that at least 89 of the 119 defendants on the List should not be on the List at all–leaving only 30 released defendants with claims of actual innocence– less than ½ of 1% of the 7403 defendants sentenced to death between 1973 and 2003. Is this a crisis or just catastrophizing?

A. Background of DPIC List

The year 1972 marks the beginning of modern death penalty jurisprudence in this country. That

year, the United States Supreme Court declared all death penalty statutes unconstitutional. *Furman v. Georgia* 408 U.S. 238 (1972). The states immediately responded by enacting various statutes tailored to meet the concerns expressed in *Furman*. In 1976, the United States Supreme Court approved new death penalty laws that narrowed the class of murderers eligible for the death penalty and permitted the presentation of any mitigating evidence to justify a sentence less than death. The Court also abrogated so-called "mandatory statutes" that did not permit presentation of mitigating evidence. There is no proof that since the reinstatement of the death penalty in 1976 that an innocent person, convicted and sentenced under these statutes, has been executed. Not even the DPIC makes this claim. *Washington Times* (9/12/99).

Nonetheless, death penalty opponents claim that numerous innocent persons have been sentenced to death, only to escape that ultimate punishment when subsequently exonerated. The principal source of this claim is the DPIC List. The DPIC describes itself as "a non-profit organization serving the media and the public with analysis and information on issues concerning capital punishment." In actuality, the DPIC is an anti-death penalty organization that was established "to shape press coverage of the death penalty." *The American Spectator*, April 2000 at 21; *Washington Post* (12/9/98). Its Board of Directors is comprised of prominent anti-death penalty advocates and defense lawyers.

The DPIC List was first assembled in 1993 at the request of the House Subcommittee on Civil and Constitutional Rights. The List has its roots in a series of studies beginning with Bedau & Radelet, Miscarriages of Justice in Potentially Capital Cases, 40 *Stanford Law Rev*. 21 (1987)[hereinafter *Stanford*]. This article was followed by the 1992 publication of the book, *In Spite of Innocence*, by Bedau, Radelet, and Putnam.[4] The most recent article is Radelet, Lofquist, & Bedau, Prisoners Released from Death Rows Since 1970 Because of Doubts About Their Guilt, 13 *T.M.Cooley L. Rev*. 907 (1996)[hereinafter *Cooley*].

During 2002, the DPIC added a specific explanation of its criteria for "innocence" to the List: "The definition of innocence that DPIC uses in placing defendants on the list is that they had been convicted and sentenced to death, and subsequently either a) their conviction was overturned and they were acquitted at a re-trial, or all charges were dropped; or b) they were given an absolute pardon by the governor based on new evidence of innocence." Under its current standards, the DPIC no longer lists defendants who plead guilty to lesser charges although it has not removed defendants from the list who did enter such pleas. *Washington Times* (9/12/99); *The Record*, Bergen County, N.J., (4/14/02). The DPIC admits that actual innocence is "an unknowable fact....". *Richmond Times Dispatch* (1/19/03).

As will be shown, the DPIC's standards as a whole are inadequate, misleading, and unsatisfactory. Moreover, this recent restatement of criteria abandons the original far more narrow standards that purported to focus on genuine "wrong person" mistakes in the conviction and sentencing of defendants to Death Row utilized in the *Stanford* and *Cooley* studies.

1. The ***Stanford*** Study

The *Stanford* article presented 350 cases "in which defendants convicted of capital or potentially capital crimes in this century, and in many cases sentenced to death, have later been found to be innocent." Thus, the article included cases during the twentieth century in which the defendants were not actually sentenced to death. The *Stanford* authors acknowledged that their study was not definitive, but only based on their untested belief that a majority of neutral observers examining these cases would conclude the defendants were actually innocent. *Stanford,* at 23-24, 47-48, 74.

The article limited the cases it discussed to defendants in cases in which it was later determined no crime actually occurred or the defendants were both legally and physically uninvolved in the crimes. The focus was primarily on "wrong-person mistakes." The article did not include defendants acquitted on grounds of self-defense. *Id.* at 45. The article relied on a variety of sources, including the "unshaken conviction by the defense attorney...." that his or her client was innocent. *Id.* at 53.[5]

The *Stanford* study was criticized in Markman & Cassell, Protecting the Innocent: A Response to the Bedau-Radelet Study, 41 *Stanford L. Rev.* 121 (1988). In a reply, Bedau and Radelet acknowledged that their analyses were not definitive. Bedau & Radelet, The Myth of Infallibility: A Reply to Markman and Cassell, 41 *Stanford L. Rev.* 161, 264 (1988) [hereinafter *Stanford* Reply].

2. ***In Spite of Innocence***

The book which followed the *Stanford* study, *In Spite of Innocence* (1992), was a "less-academic" popularization of the cases presented in the *Stanford* article. The book purportedly corrected some unidentified errors from the *Stanford* article.

Significantly, *In Spite of Innocence* referred to the new post-*Furman* death penalty statutes and conceded that **"[c]urrent capital punishment law already embodies several features that probably reduce the likelihood of executing the innocent. These include abolition of mandatory death penalties, bifurcation of the capital trial into two distinct phases (the first concerned solely with the guilt of the offender, and the second devoted to the issue of sentence), and the requirement of automatic appellate review of a capital conviction and sentence."** *Id.* at 279.

The authors reiterate that the cases cited in their study include cases in which the defendant was sentenced to life or tried in non-capital jurisdictions. The study did not include cases in which the defendant was acquitted on grounds of self-defense or insanity. The study also excluded cases in which the defendant's release occurred because of due process error in trial since "[a] defendant in a capital case whose conviction rests in part on due-process error, no matter how serious or flagrant the error, is not for that reason innocent as charged." *Ibid.* at 16. To determine whether the defendant was actually innocent the authors relied on either (1) official judgments of error or (2) their unofficial judgments including reexaminations of the cases by students, journalists, or scholars who conclude that the defendant "cannot be guilty". *Id.* at 17.

In Spite of Innocence identifies "416 cases in which the wrong person was convicted of murder (or of capital rape and then sentenced to death) in the United States so far in this century. All together, roughly a third of the defendants whose cases we discuss were not merely convicted, but also sentenced to death." *Ibid.* at 17.[6]

3. The ***Cooley*** Article

The recent *Cooley* article is the principal source for the DPIC List.[7] Two of its authors, Bedau & Radelet, also wrote the original *Stanford* study and *In Spite of Innocence*. The *Cooley* article ostensibly continued the *Stanford* focus of identifying "factually innocent" defendants–wrongly convicted persons who were not actually involved in the crime.*Cooley,* at 911.

Cooley, however, had a narrower time focus than the *Stanford* article or *In Spite of Innocence*. The *Cooley* list of 68 condemned, but allegedly innocent prisoners is supposedly limited "to cases since 1970 in which serious doubts about the guilt of a death row inmate have been acknowledged." *Cooley*, at 911. The "admittedly somewhat arbitrary" cutoff date of 1970 appears to be directed at eliminating cases that were disposed of no earlier than 1973, after *Furman v. Georgia,* 408 U.S. 238 (1972). *Cooley*, at 911 fn. 27. As the authors had indicated in their earlier book, *In Spite of Innocence*, current death penalty law included features that probably reduced the likelihood that an innocent person would be sentenced to death. Accordingly, earlier cases under old statutes would not add much to analyzing the contemporary problem of "wrongful convictions". Nevertheless, the *Cooley* cutoff date of 1970 was still flawed for purposes of assessing our current capital punishment system since it still included prisoners convicted under the pre-1972, pre-*Furman* statutes.

The *Cooley* article purported not to include inmates released because of "due process errors" unrelated to allegations of innocence. *Cooley*, at 911-912. Finally, *Cooley* excluded inmates who were found to be guilty of lesser included homicides or not guilty by reason of mental defenses. *Cooley*, at 912-913.

However, *Cooley* expanded the original *Stanford* study to include allegedly "innocent" defendants who actually committed the crime or were involved in the murder. Unlike the *Stanford* article, *Cooley* included cases in which the defendant was ultimately acquitted on grounds of self defense. *Cooley*, at 913. The *Cooley* article also included cases in which defendants *pled* to lesser charges and were released "because of strong evidence of innocence." *Id.* at 914. The DPIC has since disavowed inclusion of cases in which prisoners pled to lesser charges, although it has not removed such prisoners from its List.

The *Cooley* article failed to mention at least one significant change from the previous studies--the inclusion of accomplices mistakenly convicted as actual perpetrators. The *Stanford* study excluded such defendants. "We also do not consider a defendant innocent simply because he can demonstrate, in a case of homicide, it was not he but a co-defendant who fired the fatal shot . . . because the law does not nullify the [accomplice's] culpability merely because he was not the triggerman, we do not treat him as innocent." *Stanford*, at 43. *Cooley* and the DPIC List abandoned that limitation and included supposedly innocent defendants who were still culpable as accomplices to the actual triggerman. Thus, unlike its predecessor studies, *Cooley* cited cases in which there were no actual "wrong person" mistakes–a practice which the DPIC has continued.

Finally, **and most importantly**, *Cooley* "includ[ed] cases where juries have acquitted, or state appellate courts have vacated, the convictions of defendants because of doubts about their guilt **(even if we personally believe the evidence of innocence is relatively weak).**" *Cooley*, at 914. [emphasis added]. However, except for defendant Samuel Poole, *Cooley* does not otherwise identify the defendants which the authors themselves believe have relatively weak evidence of innocence. Nevertheless, as will be noted below, a comparison of the *Cooley* list with the names omitted from the *Stanford* study and *In Spite of Innocence* suggests which cases even the authors of the *Cooley* article believe only have "weak" evidence of innocence.

Thus, the *Cooley* article and the DPIC List differ from the original *Stanford* article and *In Spite of Innocence* because they both expand the categories of allegedly innocent defendants. The *Stanford* article was "primarily concerned with wrong-person mistakes" and only included defendants whom the authors believed were legally and physically uninvolved in the crimes. *Stanford*, at 45. As will be shown, neither *Cooley* nor the DPIC List conforms to these original limitations. The result is a padded list of allegedly innocent Death Row defendants that overstates the frequency of wrongful convictions in capital cases.

4. The 2004 DPIC Publication: ***Innocence & the Crisis in the American Death Penalty***

In September 2004, the DPIC published a report entitled "Innocence & the Crisis in the American Death Penalty". This report list 116 "Inmates Exonerated and Freed from Death Row."[8] The report also reiterated and defended its criteria for including allegedly exonerated inmates on its List. According to the DPIC, its criteria are objective rather than subjective since they are based on the person's status in the legal system, e.g. the person was "acquitted" on retrial or had charges dismissed by the prosecutor or been pardoned by the executive on grounds of innocence. Nonetheless, the DPIC also conceded that it had refined its previous list and was removing six names from its list because inmates had still been convicted for some lesser offense.[2] The report concluded that there is a "crisis" in capital punishment that requires "thorough, system-wide review."

B. The DPIC List: Miscarriages of Justice or Miscarriages of Analyses?

Using the *Cooley* article as a starting point, this paper explains that as many as 89 of the 119 names on the DPIC List (as of June 24, 2005) should be eliminated. In several respects, the methodology of the DPIC List as first explained in the *Cooley* article and as later refined is deficient. The premises used in selecting and pronouncing particular defendants as "actually innocent" do not in fact support that conclusion or do not assist in determining the actual number of allegedly mistaken convictions under current capital punishment jurisprudence.

1. Time Frame: Relevance of DPIC List to Current Death Penalty Procedures

In terms of the risk of condemning the innocent to death, the "admittedly somewhat arbitrary" (*Cooley)* time frame used by the DPIC List of 1970 is over-inclusive. Although the United States Supreme Court's *Furman* decision did abrogate all of the completely discretionary, standardless death penalty statutes in 1972, it was not until 1976 that the Court upheld new death penalty statutes. As noted in the book *In Spite of Innocence*, numerous features of these new laws "probably reduce the likelihood of executing the innocent".[10]

Among the features which decreased the likelihood that an innocent person would be sentenced the death, these statutes (1) narrowed the range of death penalty eligible defendants and (2) permitted convicted murderers to produce any relevant mitigating evidence supporting a penalty less than death. Mitigating evidence may frequently include evidence that will raise so-called "residual doubt" or "lingering doubt" about the defendant's guilt or otherwise raise doubts about a defendant's level of culpability due to mental impairment or some other factor.

In 1976, the Court abrogated statutes with so-called "mandatory" death penalties which did not permit consideration of mitigating evidence. As the *Stanford* study acknowledged, it has only been since those decisions that "juries have been permitted to hear any evidence concerning the nature of the crime or defendant that would mitigate the offense and warrant a sentence of life imprisonment." These mitigating factors can include lingering doubt, mental impairments, and limited culpability. *Stanford*, at 81-83.

To the extent that the DPIC List includes defendants convicted and condemned under old statutes that did not meet the Court's 1976 standards, those defendants are irrelevant in terms of assessing contemporary capital punishment statutes and should be excluded from the List. They are irrelevant to today's system. Since those defendants were not tried under today's "guided discretion" laws, they were sentenced to death without the appropriate finding of eligibility or the opportunity to present mitigation. They were not provided the modern protections which "probably reduce the likelihood of executing the innocent." Their sentences are not reliable or pertinent indicators for evaluating the effect of **today's** statutes on the conviction and sentencing of the "actually innocent." There is no assurance they would have been sentenced to death under today's statutes.

Implicitly, the *Cooley* article accepted this premise by limiting its time frame to cases that were actually disposed of after the 1972 *Furman* decision. The mistake in *Cooley*, however, was in not further limiting the time frame to defendants sentenced to death after their state enacted the appropriate post-1972, post-*Furman* "guided discretion" statutes. See also Markman & Cassell, Protecting the Innocent: A Response to the Bedau-Radelet Study, *41 Stan. L. Rev*. 121, 147-152 (1988). The DPIC List does not cure this methodological mistaken.

In addition, the United States Supreme Court has from time to time invalidated other state death penalty statutes or issued rulings which would have affected the penalty procedures in various states. To the extent that those changes affected the eligibility for or selection of the penalty, it is inappropriate to include inmates who may not have had the benefit of those procedures.[11]

2. The Concept of "Actual Innocence"

To analyze the DPIC List, it is necessary to distinguish between the concepts of "actual innocence" and "legal innocence". The former is when the defendant is simply the "wrong person", not the actual perpetrator of the crime or otherwise culpable for the crime. The latter form of innocence means that the defendant cannot be legally be convicted of the crime, even if that person was the actual perpetrator or somehow culpable for the offense. The DPIC List blurs the distinction between these two concepts, implying that a "legally innocent" person was not "factually" the actual perpetrator. As a result, it includes many cases in which the defendants were not "factually innocent." See fn. 24, supra discussing *United States v. Quinones*, 205 F.Supp. 2d 256 (S.D.N.Y. 2002).

The United States Supreme Court and appellate courts have discussed the concept of "actual innocence". "Actual innocence means factual innocence, not mere legal insufficiency." *Bousley v. United States*, 523 U.S. 614 (1998). "Actual innocence" does not include claims based on intoxication or self defense. *Beavers v. Saffle*, 216 F.3d 918 (10th Cir. 2000). Proof of "actual innocence" also involves considering relevant evidence of guilt that was either excluded or unavailable at trial. *Schlup v. Delo*, 513 U.S. 298 (1995). At a minimum, any showing of actual innocence would have to be "extraordinarily high" or "truly persuasive". *Herrera v. Collins*, 506 U.S. 390 (1993).

The *Cooley* article (and the DPIC List initially)[12] purported to limit the list of the "innocent" to defendants who were "actually innocent," not just "legally innocent". However, the available information from the case material and media accounts they rely upon indicate that many defendants on the List were not "actually innocent." These are not cases in which it can be concluded that the prosecution charged the "wrong person".

As noted, the DPIC currently limits the cases on the List to those in which a prisoner has been acquitted on retrial or charges have been formally dismissed or the executive pardons on the basis of innocence. However, the DPIC List also includes other cases in which the conviction was reversed because of legally insufficient evidence .[13] As will be shown, inserting these cases on the List is misleading in terms of assessing whether truly innocent defendants have been convicted and sentenced to death and it skews the perception of the criminal justice system. In actuality, the DPIC List includes a number of "false exonerations" since it confounds the distinction between "legal innocence" and "actual innocence."

To begin with, defendants are only convicted if a jury or court finds them guilty of murder "beyond a reasonable doubt." Implicit in the "reasonable doubt" standard, of course, is that a conviction does not require "absolute certainty" as to guilt. Equally implicit, however, is that many guilty defendants will be acquitted, rather than convicted, because the proof does not eliminate all "reasonable doubt." *Smith v. Balkcom*, 660 F.2d 573, 580 (5th Cir. 1981).

When a jury acquits a defendant because the prosecution has not proven guilt beyond a reasonable doubt, that verdict does not mean that the defendant did not actually commit the crime i.e., that the defendant is "actually innocent". *Dowling v. United States*, 493 U.S. 342, 249 (1990). Even an acquittal based on self defense does no more than demonstrate the jury's determination that there was a reasonable doubt about guilt, not that the defendant was actually innocent. *Martin v. Ohio*, 480 U.S. 228, 233-234 (1987). A jury must acquit "someone who is probably guilty but whose guilt is not established beyond a reasonable doubt." *Gregg v. Georgia*, 428 U.S. 153, 225 (1976) (White, J.

conc.). An acquittal means that the defendant is "legally innocent", but not necessarily "actually innocent."

"Defendants are acquitted for many reasons, the least likely being innocence. A defendant may be acquitted even though almost every member of the jury is satisfied of his guilt if even one juror harbors a lingering doubt. A defendant may be acquitted if critical evidence of his guilt is inadmissible because the police violated the Constitution in obtaining the evidence by unlawful search or coercive interrogation . . . More remarkable is the spectacle of jury acquittal because the jury sympathizes with the defendant even though guilt clearly has been proven by the evidence according to the law set forth in the judge's instructions ." Schwartz, *"Innocence"-A Dialogue with Professor Sundby,* 41 *Hast. L.J.* 153, 154-155 *(1989) cited in* Bedau & Radelet, *1998 Law & Contemporary Problems* 105, 106 fn. 9. As the authors of *Stanford, In Spite of Innocence,* and *Cooley* agree, reversals, acquittals on retrial, and prosecutorial decisions not to retry cases are not conclusive evidence of innocence. *Stanford* Reply at 162.

Modern examples of this distinction between acquittal and innocence (or between "actual" and "legal" innocence) include O.J. Simpson who was acquitted of criminal charges, but was later found responsible for his wife's and Ron Goldman's deaths in a civil proceeding in which it was only necessary to prove his responsibility by a preponderance of the evidence. Or, to cite another recent example, the acquittal of the police officers in the Rodney King beating case obviously did not establish their "actual innocence" given their subsequent conviction in federal court for violating King's constitutional rights. Or, as an Ohio jury just demonstrated in a civil case, Dr. Sam Sheppard's acquittal in the 1960'a for murdering his wife did not mean he was actually innocent. *Cleveland Plain-Dealer* (4/13/00). The DPIC itself removed one case from its List when that supposedly innocent defendant, Clarence Smith, was convicted in federal court of charges which included the murder for which he had been acquitted in the Louisiana state court.

Furthermore, no matter how overwhelming the evidence of a defendant's guilt, the prosecution cannot appeal if a jury finds the defendant "not guilty". Nor may the prosecution retry an acquitted defendant. *Jackson v. Virginia*, 443 U.S. 307, 317 fn. 10 (1979). Due to the Double Jeopardy Clause, the People does not get a "second chance" to improve their evidence or present newly discovered evidence of guilt. The defendant, no matter how guilty, goes free. The defendant is "legally innocent", but not "actually innocent".

Similarly, if an appeals court reverses a conviction because the evidence of guilt was legally insufficient to prove guilt beyond a reasonable doubt, then the state cannot retry the defendant under the he Double Jeopardy Clause. *Burks v. United States*, 437 U.S. 1,

16-18 (1978). However, the judges on the appeals court cannot uphold or reverse convictions because they personally believe the convicted defendant is guilty or innocent.. Ordinarily, the judges cannot substitute their opinion for the jury's guilty verdict. They cannot second guess how the jury resolved conflicts in the evidence or the inferences the jury drew from the evidence. *Jackson v. Virginia*, 443 U.S. at 319.[14]

Thus, when an appeals court finds that the evidence was legally insufficient, it is only finding as a matter of law, not fact, that the prosecution did not present enough evidence to prove guilt beyond a reasonable doubt, i.e. the evidence of guilt was not sufficient as a matter of law for a reasonable juror to find the defendant guilty beyond a reasonable doubt. *Burks v. United States*, at 16 fn. 10. Courts will frequently be compelled legally to reverse these cases, even if the evidence signals strongly that the defendant is guilty. The defendant is "legally innocent", but not "actually innocent". The DPIC List includes cases in which the appellate court reversed a case for insufficient evidence, despite the fact that there was remaining evidence that the defendant was the actual perpetrator. These types of cases only show that the prosecution had weak cases, not that the defendant was "actually innocent". The prosecution's failure in these cases hardly justifies declaring a "crisis" in our justice system.

As will be noted in the discussions of some of the various cases on the DPIC List, some individual states themselves have their own unique and more demanding standards for sufficiency of evidence or double jeopardy. Accordingly, a reversal in one state is not representative of the potential disposition of the case under the United States Constitution or other states' laws. In other words, a prisoner may have had his case reversed for insufficient evidence in one state when that conviction might have been upheld in federal court or another state.[15]

The "reasonable doubt" standard represents the determination that the prosecution will pay the price if the evidence is insufficient and that any errors in fact-finding in criminal cases will be in favor of the defendant, i.e., that the guilty will be acquitted because of insufficient proof. *Schlup v. Delo*, 513 U.S. 298, 325 (1995); *Patterson v. New York*, 432 U.S. 197, 208 (1977). Indeed, evidence of guilt is frequently excluded and never presented to the jury if the prosecution or police have violated the defendant's constitutional rights in obtaining that evidence–even if the evidence proves the defendant's guilt. *Id.*, at 327-328.

For instance, a technical violation of the rights under *Miranda v. Arizona*, 384 U.S. 436 (1966) may lead to the exclusion of powerful evidence of guilt such as a defendant's confession or other damaging statements. If evidence is seized from the defendant in violation of the Fourth Amendment's rule against unreasonable searches and seizures, the evidence which was taken will not be presented to the jury even though that evidence demonstrates the defendant's guilt. As a result, the jury may be deprived of sufficient convincing evidence of guilt even though the defendant is undoubtedly guilty or the prosecution may no longer have sufficient evidence to try the defendant.[16]

Finally, a prosecutor's decision whether to retry a case that has resulted in a "hung jury" or has been reversed on appeal (for reasons other than lack of sufficient evidence) is not necessarily motivated by a prosecutor's personal belief that a defendant is guilty or innocent. Prosecutorial discretion is an integral part of the criminal justice system. The decision not to retry is not ipso facto a concession that the defendant is actually innocent. Rather, it frequently represents the prosecutor's professional judgment that there is simply not enough evidence to persuade an entire jury that the defendant is guilty beyond a reasonable doubt or that for some other reason, such as the fact that the defendant is now serving time for other convictions, further prosecution is not appropriate. If an earlier trial has ended in a mistrial because the jury could not unanimously agree on guilt or innocence, the prosecutor may simply conclude as a practical matter that the evidence is insufficiently compelling to persuade a jury of guilt beyond a reasonable doubt.

Local prosecutors have discretion to decide whether to seek the death penalty. That discretion is motivated by such factors as the strength of the case, the likelihood of conviction, witness and evidence problems, potential legal issues, the character of the defendant, the case's value as a deterrent to future crime, and the Government's overall law enforcement priorities. *United States v. Armstrong*, 517 U.S. 456, 463-464 (1996); *Gregg v. Georgia*, 428 U.S. 153, 225 (1976) (White, J. conc.); *People v.. Gephart*, 93 Cal.App.3d 989, 999-1000 (1979). Prosecutors have the discretion to decline to charge the defendant, to offer a plea bargain, or to decline to seek the death penalty in any particular case. *McCleskey v. Kemp*, 481 U.S. 279, 295, 311-312 (1987.)

"Numerous legitimate factors may influence the outcome of a trial and a defendant's ultimate sentence, even though they may be irrelevant to his actual guilt. If sufficient evidence to link a suspect to a crime cannot be found, he will not be charged. The capability of the responsible law enforcement agency can vary widely. Also, the strength of the available evidence remains a variable throughout the criminal justice process and may influence a prosecutor's decision to offer a plea bargain or go to trial. Witness availability, credibility, and memory also influence the results of prosecutions." *McCleskey*, at 306-307 fn. 28. As even the authors of the *Stanford* study concede, "[p]rosecutors sometimes fail to retry the defendant after a reversal not because of doubt about the accused's guilt, much less because of belief that the defendant is innocent or that the defendant is not guilty `beyond a reasonable doubt', but for reasons wholly unrelated to guilt or innocence." 1998 *Law & Contemporary Problems* at 106. When a conviction is reversed, this discretion will also be affected by the toll that the passage of time has taken on the witnesses and the evidence. *United States v. Mechanik*, 475 U.S. 66, 72 (1986).[17] The DPIC criteria fail to take these factors into account.

3. Timing of "Exonerations": Not on Death Row

The DPIC List is subtitled "Released from Death Row". The implicit message is that the List contains inmates who have been found innocent while serving a sentence of death. However, several of the prisoners identified on the List were no longer under sentence of death and no longer residing on Death Row when they were "exonerated". These defendants successfully sought reversal of their initial convictions or sentences on review. When they were retried, they were either acquitted, convicted of lesser crimes[18], or sentenced to punishments less than death.

The criminal justice system provides many procedural protections for defendants. As already noted, courts actually exclude evidence of guilt that was seized in violation of a defendant's constitutional rights. At trial, jurors cannot be excluded because of race or gender. Jury voir dire is carefully directed at uncovering bias based on attitudes about the death penalty or race. Incriminating statements by separately tried co-defendants are inadmissible at trial. The admission and exclusion of potentially inflammatory evidence is subject to the discretion of the trial court based on considerations of reliability, relevance, and prejudice. The defendant is entitled to the effective assistance of counsel. The prosecution is obligated to provide timely discovery and to disclose any evidence that could materially assist the defendant's defense. The prosecution is also subject to limits as to the extent it can go in arguing its case to the jury. In capital cases, the juries consider any relevant mitigating evidence the defendants present. Defendants have the opportunity to raise new issues relating to newly-discovered evidence by motions for new trial addressed to the trial court.

These trials are reviewed by a dual system of review "unique" to the United States. Louis Powell, Capital Punishment, 102 *Harv. L. Rev.* 1035, 1045 (1989). Reviewing courts determine if there was sufficient evidence to support a conviction and whether prejudicial error occurred. These courts reverse the defendants' convictions and sentences if the error could have made a difference in their trials' outcome. In fact, the conviction is not actually considered "final" until this direct review is

finished. At times, when errors are corrected on retrial, defendants are either acquitted or receive a sentence less than death. These are cases in which the "conventional system of appellate review worked." 86 *Judicature* 83, 88 (September-October 2002).

The DPIC List includes cases involving such defendants. However, its failure to account for reversals of convictions or sentences based on errors related to these protections is another flaw in its methodology. It is, in fact, complete speculation whether or not defendants whose convictions and sentences were reversed would have been sentenced to death if their first trial had not been marred by trial error that was remedied through our extensive legal review system.

The DPIC List includes defendants who were either acquitted or received sentences less than death after their initial convictions and sentences were reversed.[19] When defendants' convictions and sentences are reversed for trial errors and the defendants receive a second death sentence or are even acquitted on retrial, the inference is that the defendants should never have served time on Death Row and that the system has appropriately and fairly made that ultimate determination. At this point, it is not a matter of happenstance or accident that the "innocent" defendants are released from Death Row. In these cases, the "innocent" defendant is no longer on Death Row at all. The fact that a defendant was mistakenly convicted or sentenced to death at a first trial due to a "trial error" which was then corrected to his benefit on retrial does not provide much support for a claim that "actually innocent" defendants are being erroneously sent to Death Row. A reviewing system has been established to detect the inevitable errors that occur in a system which will always have elements of fallibility. When that system works, it is hardly fair or accurate to use cases reversed and rectified under that system as reasons to criticize the accuracy of that system. [20]

To the extent that the List has any value at all-that value is in assessing the dangers of sentencing innocent people to Death Row under the current death penalty system. When the review system works and a defendant's life is spared because he or she is acquitted or sentenced to a lesser punishment, the fact that that defendant is later "exonerated" does little to advance the case that there is an unacceptable risk of innocent people being sent to Death Row for execution. The system itself prevented that from happening. Yet, the DPIC includes exactly those types of cases on its List.[21]

It is submitted that for purposes of evaluating the accuracy of the current system of capital punishment in the United States, it is inappropriate to include defendants who are already permanently removed from Death Row due to their success in the review process. These are not innocent defendants who were in danger of being executed at the time of their exoneration. Absent the original trial error that led to the reversals of their initial convictions and sentences, it is total conjecture whether they would have been sent to Death Row at all.[22]

C. Cases on DPIC List: Actually Innocent or Falsely Exonerated While on Death Row?

After examination of the DPIC List and available supporting materials including appellate opinions, newspaper reports, and academic articles, it is submitted that the following 89 defendants should be stricken from the current DPIC List of 119 allegedly innocent defendants "freed from Death Row."[23]

The DPIC List fails to take into account many of the factors mentioned above that may lead to an acquittal or a prosecutorial decision not to retry a case even though a defendant is not actually innocent. As a result, it includes defendants whose guilt is debatable to say the least and whom it is hard to believe that a majority of neutral observers would conclude were innocent or not actual perpetrators. (the same standard used in the original *Stanford* study that formed the basis for the List). The List also includes cases that should not be considered in terms of assessing the overall effectiveness of today's post-1972 death penalty procedures in reliably and accurately imposing the ultimate punishment on defendants who legitimately deserve that sanction, procedures that "probably reduce the likelihood of executing the innocent." Such cases include defendants who were convicted under archaic death penalty statutes and who were freed after the appellate system properly functioned to return their cases for retrial due to prejudicial trial error.

A fundamental precept of death penalty law is that each case should include an "individualized inquiry" into the circumstances of the offense and the offender. *McCleskey,* 481 U.S. at 303. Yet, the DPIC does not apply this precept to the cases on its own List. Rather, it basically concludes that a defendant is "innocent" if he is not convicted in a retrial or the charges are dismissed by the prosecutor. This overinclusive criteria is not supported by either law or experience. It demonstrates that "a consistency produced by ignoring individual differences is a false consistency." *Eddings v. Oklahoma*, 455 U.S. 104, 112 (1982). [24]

For ease of cross-referencing, the cases which should be omitted from the DPIC List are discussed in the same numerical order as they currently appear on the DPIC's website.[25]

1. **David Keaton**--Conviction and sentence occurred prior to 1972 (pre-modern death penalty statute era). *Anderson v. Florida*, 267 So.2d 8 (Fla. 1972).

2. **Samuel A. Poole**--Convicted of rape and sentenced under a defunct mandatory sentencing law which precluded consideration of mitigating evidence. *Woodson* v. *North Carolina* (1976) 428 U.S. 280. The United States Supreme Court has also declared the the death penalty for rape to be cruel and unusual punishment. *Coker v. Georgia*, 433 U.S. 584 (1977). Moreover, *Cooley* concedes that evidence of Poole's innocence is "weak". *Cooley*, at 917.

3. **Wilbur Lee &**

4. **Freddie Pitts**--Conviction and sentence occurred prior to 1972. *In re Bernard R. Baker*, 267 So.2d 331 (Fla. 1972).

5. **James Creamer**–Creamer was sentenced to death for a 1971 murder. According to Cobb County court records, his initial death sentence was imposed on February 4, 1973, but was then reduced to life on September 28, 1973. This reduction is understandable since the Georgia death penalty law had been declared unconstitutional in 1972 in *Furman*. *Creamer v. State*, 205 S.E.2d 240 (Ga. 1974) (Creamer sentenced to four consecutive life terms); *Emmett v. Ricketts*, 397 F.Supp. 1025 (N.D.Ga. 1975). There was some initial confusion about the actual sentence in this case since the original Stanford study and the reviewing courts' decisions simply stated that Creamer had received a life sentence. Of course, Creamer's case is not relevant to assessing today's post-*Furman* capital punishment system.

6. **Christopher Spicer**- This recent addition to the DPIC List is irrelvant. He was sentenced under the unconstitutional mandatory North Carolina death penalty statute. *Woodson v. North Carolina,* 428 U.S. 280, 304 (1976).

7. **Thomas Gladish &**

8. **Richard Greer &**

9. **Ronald Keine &**

10. **Clarence Smith** --These four defendants were tried and convicted under New Mexico's invalid mandatory death penalty law which precluded consideration of mitigating evidence. *State v. Beaty,* 553 P.2d 688 (N.M.1976). It is complete speculation whether they would have been sentenced to death under a "guided discretion" statute.

11. **Delbert Tibbs**--*Tibbs v. State,* 337 So.2d 788 (Fla. 1976) (*Tibbs I*); *State v. Tibbs,* 370 So.2d 386 (Fla.App. 1979) (*Tibbs II*); *Tibbs v. State,* 397 So.2d 1120, 1123 (Fla. 1981) (*Tibbs III*); *Tibbs v. Florida,* 457 U.S. 31 (1982) (*Tibbs IV*). Tibbs was convicted of raping a woman and murdering her boyfriend. The chief witness was the surviving rape victim who identified Tibbs as her boyfriend's murderer.

Tibbs' conviction was reversed by a 4-3 vote of the Florida Supreme Court. The majority applied an anachronistic review standard that "carefully scrutinized" the testimony of the prosecutrix since she was the sole witness in the rape case "so as to avoid an unmerited conviction." *Tibbs I* at 790. The conviction was not even reversed because the Florida court found the evidence legally insufficient, but merely because the Florida court found the "weight" of the evidence was insubstantial. The court found the prosecutrix's testimony to be doubtful when compared with the lack of evidence (other than her eyewitness testimony) that Tibbs was in the area where the rape-murder occurred. *Id.* at 791.

Subsequently, in a later opinion, the Florida Supreme Court repudiated this "somewhat more subjective" rule that permitted an appellate court to reverse a conviction because of the weight of the evidence, rather than its sufficiency. In hindsight, the Florida Supreme Court candidly conceded that it should not have reversed Tibbs' conviction since the evidence was legally sufficient. *Tibbs III* at 1126. The old review standard applied to Tibbs' original case was a throwback to the long discarded rule that a rape conviction required corroboration of the rape victim's testimony–an unenlightened rule which inherently distrusted the testimony of the rape victim. *Id.* at 1129 fn. 3 (Sundberg, C.J. dis. & conc.); *see e.g. People v. Rincon-Pineda,* 14 Cal.3d 864 (Cal. 1975). The reversal of Tibbs' conviction was a windfall for Tibbs, not a finding of innocence.

Subsequently, a debate in the Florida courts as to whether or not Tibbs could be retried under the Double Jeopardy Clause made its way to the United States Supreme Court.

Justice O'Connor's opinion explained that the rape victim gave a detailed description of her assailant and his truck. Tibbs was stopped because he matched her description of the murderer. The victim had already viewed photos of several single suspects on three or four occasions and had not identified them. She examined several books of photos without identifying any suspects. However, when she saw Tibbs' photo, she did identify Tibbs as the rapist-murderer. She again identified Tibbs in a lineup and positively identified him at trial. *Tibbs IV* at 33 & fn. 2. At trial, the victim admitted drug use and that she used drugs "shortly" before the crimes occurred. She was confused as to the time of day that she first met Tibbs. Although not admitted as evidence, polygraphs showed however that the victim was truthful. Tibbs denied being in the area during the time of the offense and his testimony was partially corroborated. However, the prosecution introduced a card with Tibbs' signature which contradicted his testimony as to his location. Tibbs disputed that he had signed the card. *Id.* at 34-35. O'Connor's opinion also noted the evidence that the Florida Supreme Court had originally believed weakened the prosecution's case. However, since the evidence of guilt was not legally insufficient, the Double Jeopardy Clause did not bar Tibbs' retrial. *Id.* at 35.

Ultimately, due to the current status of the surviving victim--a lifelong drug addict--the original prosecutor concluded the evidence was too tainted for retrial. *In Spite of Innocence,* at 59. Nonetheless, the evidence recounted in the United States Supreme Court decision hardly supports a claim that Tibbs is actually innocent.

The state prosecutor who chose not to retry Tibbs recently explained to the Florida Commission on Capital Crimes that Tibbs "was never an innocent man wrongfully accused. He was a lucky human being. He was guilty, he was lucky and now he is free."

13. **Jonathan Treadaway--** *State v. Treadaway*, 568 P.2d 1061, 1063-1065 (Ariz. 1977); *State v. Corcoran (Treadaway I)* 583 P.2d 229 (Ariz. 1978) (*Treadaway II*). Treadaway was convicted of the sodomy and first degree murder of a young boy in the victim's bedroom. His conviction was reversed and he was acquitted on retrial.

Treadaway's two palmprints were found outside a locked bedroom window of the victim's home. When Treadaway was arrested, he had no explanation for these palmprints. Treadaway admitted being a peeping tom in the victim's neighborhood, but did not remember ever looking in the victim's house. He denied being at the victim's house the night of the murder. However, the victim's mother testified she washed the windows the day before the murder, "raising an inference that the palm prints found on the morning after the murder [were] fresh" and also raising the inference that Treadaway was lying. Pubic hairs on the victim's body were similar to Treadaway's. His conviction was reversed by the Arizona Supreme Court in a 3-2 decision because the trial court erroneously admitted evidence that Treadaway committed sex acts with a 13-year old boy three years before the murder.

When Treadaway's retrial began, the Arizona Supreme Court reviewed several pretrial evidentiary rulings. It admitted evidence that Treadaway sexually attacked and tried to strangle a boy three months before the murder at issue in the boy's bedroom. However, the court excluded the interrogation in which Treadaway failed to explain his palmprints outside the victim's bedroom window, specifically refused to provide information any information, and made other incriminating statements. The exclusion was based on the police failure to comply with the technical requirements of the *Miranda* decision, not because Treadaway's statements or failure to explain the palmprints on the window were somehow unreliable or involuntary.

This decision to exclude Treadaway's interrogation was a crucial difference between his two trials. Although there was defense evidence that the victim died of natural causes, the jurors who acquitted Treadaway on retrial later stated that they were actually concerned about the lack of evidence that Treadaway had been inside the boy's home. *Stanford*, at 164; *In Spite of Innocence*, at 349. Therefore, Treadaway's failure to explain the palmprints at the window could have been critical evidence since those palmprints at the very least would have connected Treadaway with a location just outside the boy's home on the night of the murder. Treadaway's inability to explain the suspicious presence to the police of his fingerprints would ordinarily indicate a "consciousness of guilt" about his presence at the boy's home. However, the jury was never permitted to know that Treadaway had had no explanation for those palmprints–a circumstance consistent with his guilt. Thus, significant probative evidence of Treadaway's consciousness of guilt about the palmprints on the windowsill, directly relevant to the jury's concern about the case, was never disclosed to the jury at his second trial. Since it cannot be known what the impact of that excluded evidence would have been on the second jury, Treadaway's acquittal on retrial did not demonstrate that he was innocent.

Furthermore, in light of the recent United States Supreme Court decision in *Ring v. Arizona* it is speculation whether a jury would have found Treadaway eligible to be sentenced to death.

14. **Gary Beeman**--Convicted and sentenced under Ohio's invalid death penalty statute which limited mitigating evidence. *Lockett v. Ohio*, 438 U.S. 586 (1978). Accordingly, it is speculative that he would have received a death sentence under appropriate law.

17. **Charles Ray Giddens**--In 1981, the Oklahoma appellate court reversed Giddens' conviction for insufficient evidence, not actual innocence, because the testimony of his alleged accomplice was "replete with conflicts". In 1982, the state court held that retrial was barred under the Double Jeopardy Clause. *In Spite of Innocence*, at pp. 306-307. Thus, this was a case in which the evidence was found insufficient to prove guilt, not a case in which the defendant was exonerated.

18. **Michael Linder**–This defendant was acquitted on retrial based on grounds of self-defense. *Cooley*, at 948. Thus, this was not a case involving a "wrong person" mistake as originally defined in the *Stanford* study.

19. **Johnny Ross**-- *People v. Ross*, 343 So.2d 722 (La. 1977). This defendant's name should be removed since he was sentenced under the unconstitutional mandatory Louisiana death penalty statute which precluded consideration of mitigating evidence.

20. **Ernest (Shujaa) Graham**-Another recent addition to the DPIC List who was sentenced under California's invalid mandatory death penalty statute. *Graham v. Superior Court*, 98 Cal.App.3d 880 (1980).

21. **Annibal Jaramillo**--*Jaramillo v. State*, 417 So.2d 257 (Fla. 1982). This defendant's double murder conviction and death judgment were reversed for legal insufficiency of evidence. The male victim had been bound with cord and then shot. Near the body was a coil of cord and near that coil was the packaging for a knife. Jaramillo's fingerprint was found on the packaging and the knife, but not on the knife wrapper. A nearby grocery bag had Jaramillo's fingerprint. Jaramillo testified that he was helping the victims' nephew stack boxes in the garage the day before the murder. He asked for a knife to help cut the boxes. The nephew directed him inside to a grocery bag with a knife. According to Jaramillo, he removed the knife from the wrapper and returned to the garage. He claimed he later left the knife on the dining room table where it was found after the murder. Thus, Jaramillo's testimony conveniently explained the fingerprints on the incriminating objects. According to the recent report of the Florida Commission on Capital Cases, the victims' nephew who could have either corroborated or contradicted Jaramillo's version of events was unavailable to testify at trial since his whereabouts were unknown.

Although there was circumstantial evidence of Jaramillo's guilt in the double murder, the conviction could not be sustained under Florida law unless the evidence was inconsistent with any reasonable hypothesis of innocence. Proof of Jaramillo's fingerprints on several items at the scene associated with the murder was not inconsistent with Jaramillo's reasonable explanation of the fingerprints (helping the nephew stack boxes in the garage).

This Florida case illustrates a key point about our federal-state criminal justice system. Florida's "sufficiency of evidence" rule in this case was more stringent than the standard required under the Federal Constitution and applied by the majority of other states. See, e.g., *Fox v.* State, 469 So.2d 800, 803 (Fla.App. 1985); *Geesa v. State*, 820 S.W.2d 154, 161 fn. 9 (Tex.Crim. 1991). Ordinarily, it is not necessary for the prosecution to eliminate every hypothesis other than guilt. *Jackson v. Virginia*, 443 U.S. 307, 326 (1979). Thus, in both federal court and the majority of states, the evidence would have been sufficient to support Jaramillo's conviction notwithstanding his alternative explanation for his fingerprints. The presence of Jaramillo's fingerprints on items associated with the murder would have been sufficient for conviction. See, e.g., *Taylor v. Stainer*, 31 F.3d 907 (9th Cir. 1994); *Schell v. Witek*, 218 F.3d 1017 (9th Cir. en banc 2000).

However, under Florida law, Jaramillo's innocent explanation was not inconsistent with the presence of the fingerprints on those objects. Accordingly, under state law, the conviction was reversed since Jaramillo's innocent explanation for the prints could not be eliminated. The Florida Commission on Capital Cases described this case as an "execution-style" robbery and noted information that Jaramillo was a Colombian "hitman". Jaramillo was subsequently deported to Colombia, where he was murdered. It was the opinion of local law enforcement that Jaramillo "got away with a double homicide."

22. **Lawyer Johnson**--Convicted under pre-*Furman* death penalty law in Massachusetts. *Stewart v. Massachusetts*, 408 U.S. 845 (1972); *Commonwealth v. O'Neal*, 339 N.E.2d 676 (Mass. 1975); *Limone v. Massachusetts*, 408 U.S. 936 (1972).

25. **Clifford Henry Bowen**--*Behrens v. State*, 699 P.2d 156 (Okla. 1985); *Bowen v. State*, 715 P.2d 1093 (Okla. 1984); *Bowen v. Maynard*, 799 F.2d 593 (10th Cir. 1986). The federal court granted relief on a claim that the prosecution failed to disclose evidence of an alternative suspect. However, Bowen was not retried due to the death of a prosecution witness. *Tulsa World* (9/24/00).

26. **Joseph Green Brown**--*Brown v. State*, 381 So.2d 690 (Fla. 1980); *Brown v. State*, 439 So.2d 872 (Fla. 1983); *Brown v. Wainwright*, 785 F.2d 1457 (11th Cir. 1986). Brown was convicted and sentenced to death based primarily on the testimony of potential accomplice Ronald Floyd, a witness who subsequently went through a series of recantations and retractions of his recantations. Associate Justice Brennan actually relied on Brown's case to note: **"Recantation testimony is properly viewed with great suspicion."** *Dobbert v. Wainwright*, 468 U.S. 1231 (1984) (Brennan, J. dis.) (citing *Brown v. State*, 381 So.2d 690). Brown was not granted a retrial because Floyd's testimony implicating Brown was false, but because Floyd and the prosecution did not disclose that Floyd was testifying in return for an agreement that he would not be prosecuted in the case. Floyd initially flunked a polygraph test about his general involvement in the murder, but then passed the test three times in terms of whether or not he was an actual perpetrator in the crime. However, Floyd also recanted his testimony implicating Brown, then recanted that recantation during an evidentiary hearing. Subsequently, Floyd again repudiated his initial trial testimony and the prosecution was unable to retry Brown. Given the inherent unreliability of the sequence of Floyd's multiple recantations (which are "properly viewed with great suspicion"), Brown cannot be deemed actually innocent.

27. **Perry Cobb &**

28. **Darby Williams**-- *People v. Cobb et al.*, 455 N.E.2d 31 (Ill. 1983). The convictions and death sentences of these co-defendants were reversed for a variety of instructional and evidentiary errors. They were acquitted on retrial. It is speculation whether they would have been convicted and sentenced to death initially absent the "trial errors" that occurred at their first trial.

29. **Vernon McManus**–*McManus v. State*, 591 S.W.2d 505 (Tex. 1980). McManus' conviction was reversed because of jury selection issues unrelated to his guilt or innocence. Ultimately, the prosecution chose not to retry the case because a witness refused to testify, but there were no widespread allegations of innocence. Accordingly, his case was not even included in the *Cooley* article as an "actually innocent" defendant. *Cooley,* at 912.

30. **Anthony Ray Peek**--*Peek v. State*, 488 So.2d 52 (Fla. 1986). Peek was acquitted after his two prior convictions for this 1977 murder were reversed for various evidentiary errors, including the admission of an unrelated rape. He was prosecuted for raping and strangling to death an elderly woman in her home. She lived a mile from the halfway house where Peek resided. Her car was found also found abandoned even nearer the halfway house. Two of Peek's fingerprints were lifted from inside the victim's car window. Blood and seminal stains on the victim's bedclothes were consistent with Peek's identity as a type-O secretor. A hair with features similar to Peek's was recovered in a cut stocking in the victim's garage area. Peek claimed that his fingerprints got on the victim's car when he was out of his halfway house in the morning and tried to burglarize her abandoned car. Peek presented evidence that the periodic night checks at the halfway house did not indicate any unauthorized absences the night of the murder.

The acquittal represents a finding of reasonable doubt, not actual innocence. Prosecutors attributed the acquittal to the passage of time and loss of evidence. In particular, the state attorney told the Florida Commission on Capital Cases: "Mr. Peek is also on the List, as are several others from other circuits who got new trials and then were acquitted. I fail to see the rationale for including these people."

31. **Juan Ramos**–*Ramos v. State*, 496 So.2d 121 (Fla. 1986). Ramos's conviction was reversed on state appeal because of improper introduction of dog scent lineup identification evidence. The court found a lack of foundation that dog scent identification was reliable and questioned the fairness of the particular dog scent identification lineup in this case. Without a fair and reliable dog scent identification, no other forensic evidence tied Ramos to the crime and he was acquitted on retrial. It should be noted that with proper foundation that dog scent lineup identifications are admissible evidence in many states. *Winston v. State*, 78 S.W.2d 522 (Tex.Crim.App. 2002) and cases cited therein; *People v. Mitchell*, 110 Cal.App.4th 772 (2003); *People v. Willis*, 115 Cal.App.4th 379 (2004). This case is an example of when a conviction and sentence have been reversed under the system of appellate review and the defendant is then acquitted in a properly

tried case. As such, its inclusion on the DPIC List does not advance the argument about the hazards of sentencing innocent defendants to death.

32. **Robert Wallace**--Acquitted on retrial based on either self defense or accidental shooting defense. Accordingly, this is not a "wrong person" mistake.

33. **Richard Neal Jones**--*Jones v. State*, 738 P.2d 525 (Okla.Crim. 1987). Jones' defense was that he was passed out in a car while three other men beat up the victim, shot him, and threw his weighted body in the river. Jones' conviction was reversed in a 2-1 decision because the trial court erroneously admitted incriminating post offense statements by Jones' non-testifying codefendants, a violation of the hearsay rule. The dissent noted that the only hearsay statement which actually implicated Jones should still should have been admitted as a prior consistent statement. At the very least, Jones was present at the murder scene and a party to the conspiracy leading to the murder. Accordingly, he would not have been considered "actually innocent" under the standards of the original *Stanford* study. His culpability would appear to be no less than that of the actual murderers. See *Mann v. State*, 749 P.2d 115 (1988); *Thompson* v. *Oklahoma*, 487 U.S. 815, 817, 859 (1988); *Thompson v. State*, 724 P.2d 780 (Okla. Crim. App. 1986) (separate trial of co-defendant with evidence directly implicating Jones).

34. **Willie A. Brown &**

35. **Larry Troy**– *Brown v. State & Troy v. State*, 515 So.2d 211 (Fla. 1987). This is a prison murder. Three inmates testified against Brown and Troy. At least one defense witness was impeached with prior statements implicating Brown and Troy. The convictions of these two defendants were reversed because of a prosecutorial discovery error–the failure to timely disclose a prior taped statement by a witness which contradicted another state witness. Ultimately, the state dropped charges because one of the prison witnesses recanted. However, the witness made the offer to recant his testimony against Brown to Brown's girlfriend in return for $2000. *Cooley*, at 930. The "recantation for hire" hardly inspires confidence that Brown and Troy are "actually innocent."

36. **Randall Dale Adams**– *Adams v. Texas*, 448 U.S. 38 (1980). This is a notorious case made famous by the film documentary *The Thin Blue Line*. However, Adams' death sentence had been reversed by the United States Supreme Court because of the court had erroneously excluded jurors who were not favorable to the death penalty. Rather than conducting a complete retrial, as a matter of expediency, the Governor of Texas commuted Adams' sentence to life imprisonment. Thus, Adams was not on Death Row when he was later exonerated and his death sentence had been reversed because of errors

directly relating to the imposition of the death penalty in the first place. Radelet & Zsembik, Executive Clemency in Post-Furman Capital Cases 27 *U.Rich.L.Rev.* 289 (1993).

37. **Robert Cox**--*Cox v. State*, 555 So.2d 352 (Fla. 1990). This first degree murder conviction was reversed for insufficient evidence, not because of innocence. "Circumstances that create nothing more than a strong suspicion that the defendant committed the crime was not sufficient to support a conviction . . . Although state witnesses cast doubt on Cox' alibi, the state's evidence could have created only a suspicion, rather than proving beyond a reasonable doubt, that Cox, and only Cox, murdered the victim." Again, this case is an example of a reversal due to Florida's more stingent legal sufficiency standard for proof beyond a reasonable doubt. The evidence obviously still indicated a "strong suspicion" of Cox's guilt.

38. **Timothy Hennis**–*State v. Hennis*, 372 S.E.2d 523 (N.C. 1988). The conviction and death sentence was reversed on appeal because the trial court erroneously admitted multiple autopsy photos. Hennis was acquitted on retrial. It is speculation whether he would have been sentenced to death at all absent the initial trial court error.

39. **James Richardson**--*Richardson v. State*, 546 So.2d 1037 (Fla. 1989). Convicted and sentenced under invalid pre-*Furman* statute in Florida.

41. **John C. Skelton**--*Skelton v. State*, 795 S.W.2d 162 (Tex.Crim.App. 1989). In a 2-1 split decision, the Texas appeals court was reversed the capital murder conviction for insufficient evidence of guilt beyond a reasonable doubt. The majority opinion believed there was a possibility that another person committed the murder. Nevertheless, the majority explained: "Although the evidence against appellant **leads to a strong suspicion or probability** that appellant committed the capital offense, we cannot say that it excludes to a moral certainty every other reasonable hypothesis except appellant's guilt . . . Although this Court does not relish the thought of reversing the conviction in this heinous case and ordering an acquittal, because the evidence does not exclude every other reasonable hypothesis, we are compelled to do so." [emphasis added]. The dissent outlines the evidence of a "strong suspicion" of Skelton's guilt. Once again, this reversal is based on a stringent standard of evidentiary sufficiency not required by the United States Constitution and no longer even applied in Texas. This appears to be another of the "relatively weak" innocence cases not included in *In Spite of Innocence.* The reversal of Skelton's conviction was not a finding of "actual innocence".

42. **Dale Johnston**– *State v. Johnston,* 1986 WL 8798 (Oh.App. 1986) [2 unreported opinions]; *State v. Johnston*, 529 N.E.2d 898 (Ohio 1988); *State v. Johnston*, 580 N.E.2d 1162 (Ohio 1990). This defendant was convicted and sentenced to death for slaying his stepdaughter and her fiancé. The stepdaughter had publicly complained in the past about

incestuous advances by Johnston. A witness who had been hypnotized to refresh his recollection testified as to his pre-hypnosis recollection that he identified Johnston angrily forcing a couple into his car on or about the day of the murders. Feedbags consistent with feedbags found on Johnston's farm were also found at the gravesite of the two victims. Some bloodstained items were seized from a strip mining pit on Johnston's property. Johnston's first conviction was ultimately reversed because of some problems with the hypnotized witness and the state's failure to disclose evidence which may have helped Johnston with his defense. Prior to retrial, the court excluded incriminating statements Johnston made during his initial interrogation as well as incriminating evidence seized due to the interrogation. The prosecution then dismissed the case due to the passage of time, poor recollection of the witnesses, and the suppression of evidence. Johnston's subsequent wrongful imprisonment lawsuit was rejected since "although the evidence did not prove Johnston committed the murders, it did not prove his innocence." *Cleveland Plain Dealer* (5/11/90, 5/12/90, 6/22/91, 9/13/93); *Associated Press* (5/11/90).

43. **Jimmy Lee Mathers**-- *State v. Mathers*, 796 P.2d 866 (Ariz. 1990). Mathers was convicted, along with two codefendants, of the murder of Sterleen Hill in 1987. In a 3-2 decision, the Arizona Supreme Court reversed Mathers' conviction for insufficient evidence. Since the reversal was based on insufficiency of the evidence, retrial was barred by the Double Jeopardy Clause. The dissent points out that there was still ample evidence of Mathers' guilt even if the majority of the court did not believe there was substantial evidence to support a conviction beyond a reasonable doubt. The appellate court reversal of Mathers' conviction was not a finding of actual innocence and the record of his case would not possibly justify such a finding.

45. **Bradley Scott**--*Scott v. State*, 581 So.2d 887 (Fla.1991). This case was reversed due to delay in prosecution and insufficient circumstantial evidence. The delay in prosecution appears to have hampered both parties to the extent that no assessment may be made of Scott's actual innocence. According to the appeals court, the available circumstantial evidence "could only create a suspicion that Scott committed this murder." Once again, even if the available evidence of Scott's guilt was not sufficient to support a conviction beyond a reasonable doubt, he certainly was not exonerated.

47. **Jay C. Smith**--*Commonwealth v. Smith*, 615 A.2d 321 (Pa. 1992); *Commonwealth v. Smith*, 568 A.2d 600 (Pa.1989); *Smith v. Holtz* (3rd Cir. 2000), 210 F.3d 186; *Smith v. Holtz* (M.D.Pa. 1998) 30 F.Supp.2d 468. Smith was not freed because he was innocent, but because the Pennsylvania court believed that Pennsylvania's double jeopardy clause barred a retrial due to prosecutorial misconduct in withholding exculpatory evidence. The Pennsylvania court conceded that the United States Constitution and other states's laws would not necessarily have compelled such a harsh sanction.

Without belaboring the evidence of Smith's guilt which was unaffected by the evidence withheld by the prosecution, it is enough to note that the DPIC List does not mention Smith's subsequent loss in civil court when he sued the Commonwealth of Pennsylvania for wrongful imprisonment. As the appeals court explained, **"Our confidence in Smith's**

convictions for the murder of Susan Reinert and her two children is not the least bit diminished . . . and Smith has therefore not established that he is entitled to compensation . . . " [emphasis added]. Indeed, a federal jury trial ultimately found that the withheld evidence was not "crucial" at all and that the prosecution's alleged misconduct did not undermine confidence in the outcome of Smith's trial. Thus, if anything, the courts have repeatedly reaffirmed their conclusion that Smith was "actually guilty". Smith's inclusion on the DPIC List is a "false exoneration" at its most extreme.

48. **Kirk Bloodsworth**--*Bloodsworth v. State*, 512 A.2d 1056 (Md. 1986); *Bloodsworth v. State*, 543 A.2d 382 (Md. 1988). This is another celebrated DNA exoneration case. However, Bloodsworth was not on Death Row when he was released. Rather, his death sentence had been reversed years earlier because the prosecution failed to disclose evidence of another potential suspect. The trial court erroneously denied his motion for a new trial based on this evidence and the reviewing court reversed. On retrial, Bloodsworth was sentenced to life. It is speculative that Bloodsworth would have ever been sentenced to Death Row absent the trial court's error at the first trial denying the new trial motion.

51. **Gregory Wilhoit**–*Willhoit v. State*, 816 P.2d 545 (Okla. 1991). The defendant's conviction was reversed on appeal because his trial counsel failed to present an expert witness hired by the defendant's family to rebut the prosecution's bitemark evidence. Appellant was acquitted on retrial. It is speculative that Wilhoit would have been sentenced to death at all, but for the failure of his defense counsel at the first trial to present the expert evidence.

52. **James Robison**-- *State v. Robison*, 608 P.2d 44 (Ariz. 1980). Robison was accused of being one of three participants in the conspiracy to murder Arizona news reporter Don Bolles. The other conspirators were Adamson and Dunlap. Robison was acquitted on retrial because the jury did not believe the testimony of his accomplice, Adamson. However, the separate trial of third co-defendant Dunlap elicited evidence that Robison had received "hush money" to prevent him from revealing Dunlap's role in Bolles' murder. Dunlap admitted giving gifts and money to Robison, but only out of "friendship". At Dunlap's trial, evidence was admitted of incriminating diary entries made by Robison. Dunlap filed a new trial motion offering Robison's testimony from Robison's second trial in which Robison testified that Dunlap's gifts to him were not offered to obtain his silence. The trial court denied Dunlap's motion because it did not find Robison's testimony credible. In particular, the trial court noted that Robison had admitted at his own trial that he had lied under oath and "would have no hesitation in testifying to whatever he felt was expedient." *People v. Dunlap*, 930 P.2d 518 (Ariz.App. 1996). Robison has been subsequently convicted of plotting to murder alleged accomplice Adamson. *Arizona Republic* (12/19/93, 7/27/95). The Dunlap trial record does not support including the duplicitous Robison on a list of "actually innocent" defendants. Finally, since Robison's first conviction and sentence were evidentiary error by the trial court, it is speculative that he would have been sentenced to Death Row at all.

53. **Muneer Deeb**--*Deeb v. Texas*, 815 S.W.2d 692 (1991). The evidence indicates that Deeb was not "actually innocent," even if there was not enough evidence to convict him beyond a reasonable doubt. At his first trial, Deeb was convicted of conspiring with David Wayne Spence to murder Deeb's girlfriend, Kelley, in order to collect insurance money. However, Spence and some confederates bungled the job by accidentally murdering the wrong woman and two other people. A jailhouse informant testified that Spence told him about numerous incriminating statements by Deeb in which Deeb stated that he would benefit from Kelley's death and that Deeb asked Spence if he knew someone who would kill Kelley. One of Spence's confederates, Melendez, also testified that he was present when Spence and Deeb conspired to commit the murder. Deeb's conviction was reversed because the trial court erroneously admitted Spence's hearsay statements to the informant. Deeb was acquitted on retrial. The special prosecutor at Deeb's retrial explained that Melendez had refused to testify a second time against Deeb.

However, the jury at Deeb's second trial did not believe that Deeb was "actually innocent". After the second trial in which Deeb was found not guilty, the jury foreperson more accurately put it: "We did not say that this man was innocent of the crime. We did not say that. We just could not say that he was guilty." Deeb's case is another example of how an acquittal following a reversal on appeal does not justify a conclusion that a defendant was innocent or would have been sentenced to death at all but for the trial court error at the first trial.

Spence was tried separately for the triple murders and executed for them. Evidence was presented at Spence's trial that Spence argued with Deeb about the murder, indicating that the murder had gone awry. There was also evidence that Deeb and Spence frequently discussed whether Kelley should be killed. *Spence v. Johnson*, 80 F.3d 989, 1004 fn. 12 (5th Cir. 1996); *Dallas Morning News* (11/4/93). Thus, the record of Spence's trial also indicates that Deeb was not "actually innocent".

54. **Andrew Golden**--*Golden v. State*, 629 So.2d 109 (1994). The Florida Supreme Court felt compelled to reverse Golden's conviction for murdering his wife to collect insurance because the evidence was insufficient to prove guilt beyond a reasonable doubt, but the state court noted as follows: **"The finger of suspicion points heavily at Golden**. A reasonable juror could conclude that he more likely than not caused his wife's death." After his wife's death, Golden denied having insurance. However, it turned out he had $300,000 in insurance, was heavily in debt, and that he filed for bankruptcy after her death. There was evidence he forged his wife's signature on insurance applications. The "heavy finger of suspicion" indicates that Golden is not "innocent".

57. **Robert Charles Cruz**- *State v. Cruz*, 672 P.2d 470 (Ariz. 1983); *State v. Cruz,* 857 P.2d 1249 (Ariz. 1993). In light of the United States Supreme Court's recent decision in *Ring v. Arizona*, this Arizona case should now be deleted from the DPIC List. Pursuant to

Ring, the Arizona statute unconstitutionally denied defendants their Sixth Amendment right to a jury trial on the findings necessary for death penalty eligibility by giving that power to state trial judges. As with the earlier cases in which the defendants were tried under now defunct death penalty statutes, Arizona convictions are no longer appropriately considered in light of current death penalty jurisprudence. It is simply speculative that Cruz would have been found eligible for the death penalty by a jury under a constitutional statute.

Cruz's eligibility for the DPIC List is also speculative because he was acquitted after several reversals of his convictions and sentences for evidentiary error at trial. Prior to his acquittal, he had been nearly convicted in two mistrials and had been convicted twice. His first conviction was reversed because evidence of his ties to organized crime and other violent activities was erroneously admitted at trial and because his defense counsel refused to participate in the trial on grounds that the judge was biased against Cruz. The second conviction was reversed because of jury selection error. The jurors who acquitted Cruz explained their verdict as a matter of "reasonable doubt". "Jurors admitted that they had doubts as soon as they voted unanimously for acquittal, with some saying they walked into the courtroom with aching stomachs. Some said they were consoled by the thought that if Cruz was involved, he had spent nearly 15 years in prison." Hardly a ringing endorsement of Cruz's innocence. *Arizona Republic* (6/2/95); *Phoenix Gazette* (6/2/95, 11/7/87).

58. **Rolando Cruz &**

59. **Alejandro Hernandez**-- *People v. Cruz*, 521 N.E.2d 18 (Ill. 1988); *People v. Cruz*, 643 N.E.2d 636 (Ill. 1994); *People v. Hernandez*, 521 N.E.2d 25 (Ill. 1988); *Buckley v. Fitzsimmons*, 919 F.2d 1230 (7th Cir. 1991). These defendants were charged with the notorious abduction, rape, and murder of ten-year-old Jeanine Nicarico. Cruz was convicted and sentenced to death twice, but both judgments were reversed. During the third trial, the trial court judge lambasted the police for "sloppy" police work and accused a sheriff's deputy of lying. He then directed a verdict for Cruz and freed him before the presentation of the defense case. The trial court did acknowledge that the prosecution had "circumstantial evidence" but did not consider it sufficient to support a conviction beyond a reasonable doubt.

Hernandez's first conviction was reversed due to evidentiary error. After a hung jury ended his second trial, he was convicted in a third trial and sentenced to 80 years in prison. However, that conviction was reversed and after the court dismissed Cruz's case the prosecution dropped charges against Hernandez. Thus, Hernandez was not on Death Row at the time of his release.

During this time, another convicted murderer named Brian Dugan announced he was willing to confess to being the lone perpetrator of the Nicarico murder in return for immunity from the death penalty. Dugan himself had been sentenced to two life sentences for other sex related murders. A 1995 DNA test implicated Dugan in Nicarico's murder, but excluded Cruz and Hernandez as actual perpetrators. However, this test result did not exclude Cruz's and Hernandez's potental culpability as accomplices to Nicarico's murder.

Ultimately, after Cruz's acquittal by the court, Illinois law enforcement officers and prosecutors were prosecuted for their roles in Cruz's case. The trial court excluded evidence that after the first trial for the Nicarico murder, Cruz looked at Nicarico's sister and mouthed the words, "You're next." However, during this trial, the defense for the accused law enforcement officers attempted to link Cruz with other suspects in the murder. There was evidence which raised a question as to whether Cruz and Dugan could have lived on the same block at the time of the murder, thus raising questions as to whether Dugan acted alone. Moreover, Dugan had a relevant modus operandi for burglaries which involved accomplices. Cruz himself took the stand and contradicted his previous testimony. He also testified that he was seeing a psychiatrist about his lying! The jury was advised that scientific evidence excluded Cruz as the rapist, but did not exclude Dugan. However, the jury was also told that the scientific evidence could not exclude the possibility that Cruz was present at the Nicarico murder. The police officers were acquitted. The trial court also acquitted one of the officers of a charge that he had falsely testified about incriminating statements Cruz made in jail. Some jurors stated they believed Cruz was guilty of the Nicarico murder. Other jurors observed that they could not believe Cruz's testimony that he had not made a so-called incriminating "dream statement" to the police about the murder in which he described details of the Nicarico murder. *Chicago Daily Law Bulletin* (4/28/99;5/25/99); *Chicago Daily Herald* (4/21/99, 5/5/99, 5/26/99); *Chicago Tribune* (12/8/95;4/30/99, 5/26/99); *Chicago Sun-Times* (12/9/95; 12/10/95; 5/26/99;6/6/99); *Chicago Daily Herald* (4/21/99;6/6/99); *Associated Press* (6/5/99, 7/22/02); *State Journal-Register* (6/14/99).

The actual reliability of Dugan's confession that he was the lone murderer, including his actual motivation for that confession, is subject to question. Notwithstanding the DNA test, Dugan has nothing to lose by confessing to the Nicarico murder, but also has no incentive to implicate or "snitch off" anyone else. *People v. Cruz,* 643 N.E.2d 636-695, 676-687, 691-695 (Ill. 1994)(plur.opn. of Freeman, J.) (dis.opns. of Heiple, McMorrow, J.J.).[26]

60. **Sabrina Butler**-- *Butler v. State*, 608 So.2d 314 (Miss. 1992). Butler was convicted of murdering her infant son, Walter. She brought Walter to the hospital with severe internal injuries and gave numerous conflicting statements, including at least one version in which she admitted pushing on his protruding rectum and hitting the baby boy once in the stomach with her fist when he was crying. Other versions included statements by her that she had tried to apply CPR when the baby was not breathing.

Butler's first conviction was reversed because the prosecutor improperly commented on her failure to testify at trial. She was acquitted on retrial, but not necessarily because she was not the actual killer of her young baby. At both trials, the evidence indicated that the baby died from peritonitis, the presence of foreign substances in the abdomen. Although a witness substantiated one of Butler's versions of events about administering CPR to the baby and the coroner admitted his examination had not been thorough, the jury foreperson indicated only that the jury had a "reasonable doubt" that Butler administered the fatal blow.

There does not appear to be any witness as to what occurred prior to the CPR. The jury was not told that Butler had lost custody of another child because of abuse. Apparently, the defense provided sufficient alternative explanations for the baby's injuries to "speculate" (but not establish) that the cause of death was either SIDS or a cystic kidney disease. There does not appear to be any definitive verdict as to the cause of death. Even Butler's own attorney stated that he "doesn't know what the truth is." Butler's co-counsel indicated that at best the case should have been prosecuted as a manslaughter, hardly an endorsement of Butler's innocence. Butler's acquittal on retrial does not represent a finding that she did not administer a deadly trauma to baby Walter's abdomen. *Mississippi Clarion-Ledger* (1/22/96); *Baltimore Sun*, (1/02/96); *Washington Times* (12/30/95).

63. **Roberto Miranda-** *Miranda v. State*, 707 P.2d 1121 (Nev. 1985); *Miranda v. Clark County*, 319 F.3d 465 (9th Cir. en banc 2003) This defendant was convicted and sentenced to death for a residential robbery/murder in Las Vegas. The chief witness against Miranda was an acquaintance who allegedly drove him to the victim's house and then discovered that a blood-spattered Miranda had stabbed the victim to death because of a drug deal gone bad.. Miranda and the acquaintance took items from the victim's residence. The same acquaintance testified that he drove Miranda back to the victim's residence the next day to dispose of incriminating evidence. Miranda went to Los Angeles where another witness observed a bloodstained shirt in Miranda's suitacase. This witness testified that Miranda admitted killing a person in a drug transaction. Miranda claimed that the acquaintance was the actual murderer.

Fourteen years after Miranda's conviction and death sentence, a state court vacated the judgment in Miranda's case due to ineffective assistance of counsel because of failure to develop evidence that would have implicated and impeached the acquaintance who testified for the prosecution. The prosecutor subsequently concluded that there was insufficient evidence to reprosecute and dismissed the case. The prosecutor's decision was based on the death or unavailability of witnesses, "not the weakness of the state's case in the first place that caused it to decline to reprosecute." The prosecution still believed Miranda was "involved" in the murder. Miranda was convicted primarily based on the testimony of an accomplice and the discovery of his fingerprint on some broken glass in the victim's sink. Another witness testified that he saw Miranda in Los Angeles after the murder, that Miranda had a blood stained shirt, and he admitted murdering a man in a drug transaction. When Miranda was assigned a public defender, he flunked a polygraph test administered by the public defender's office. He is, in fact, pursuing a civil rights lawsuit alleging that the public defender did not provide effective representation because the public defender's office believed he was lying about his involvement. His trial counsel believed that Miranda showed "strong evidence of guilt and deception" and that he was involved in the murder. (2/3/03); *Dallas Morning News* (4/23/97);

64. **Gary Gauger-** *Gauger v. Hendle,* 2002 WL 31130087 (N.D.Ill. 2002). Gauger was not actually sentenced to death for murdering his parents. Although the trial court erroneously imposed a death sentence in January 1994, the court granted a motion for reconsideration and vacated the sentence less than ten months later in September 1994. The trial court found that it had not considered all the mitigating evidence and concluded that Gauger should not be sentenced to death. *People v. Bull,* 705 N.E.2d 824, 843 (Ill. 1999); *Chicago Tribune* (9/23/94). Although Gauger served a brief time on Death Row, he was not properly sentenced to death by the trial court. He should never have been sent to Death Row because the trial court did not finally sentence him to be executed. Gauger's case is an example of how consideration of mitigating evidence under current law results in a sentence less than death. Whatever the reasons for Gauger's later release from prison, he is not properly considered as an innocent person released from Death Row since his initial death sentence was not legitimately imposed under Illinois law. Accordingly, Gauger's case is not appropriate for the DPIC List.[27]

In addition, Gauger's conviction was reversed because the Illinois appellate courts found that the admission of his "confession" violated the Fourth Amendment as the fruit of an illegal arrest. Without the confession, the prosecutor did not believe Gauger could be reprosecuted.

65. **Troy Lee Jones**--*In re Jones,* 13 Cal.4th 552 (1996); *People v. Jones,* 13 Cal.4th 535 (1996). The conviction was vacated because of ineffective assistance of counsel. The California Supreme Court held that while the evidence of Jones' guilt was not overwhelming, it still suggested Jones' guilt. Jones was convicted of murdering Carolyn Grayson in order to prevent Grayson from implicating him in the murder of an elderly woman, Janet Benner.

Grayson had told Jones' brother Marlow that she had seen Jones strangle the old lady. Grayson had told her daughter Sauda that Jones killed Ms. Benner. Jones' sister overheard a conversation between Jones and his mother in which Jones arguably regretted not killing Grayson when he killed Benner. The same sister also testified to Jones' involvement in a family plot to murder Grayson. Although there was also evidence that Jones was ambivalent about killing Grayson, there was more testimony that Grayson's neighbor witnessed a violent altercation between Grayson and Jones in which she assured him that she would not say anything and he continued to threaten to kill her. Grayson's body was later found in a field the day after she had reportedly left with Jones for Oakland. At best, Jones only had evidence to contradict the inferences suggesting his guilt.

To sum up: "[T]he prosecution introduced . . . evidence that [Jones] was observed attacking Carolyn Grayson with a tire iron a few weeks before she was fatally shot,

[Jones] and his family engaged in a plot to fatally poison Grayson, [Jones] confided to his brother that he had to kill Grayson or she would send him to the gas chamber, [Jones] informed his brother of the need to establish an alibi for the evening Grayson was murdered, and Grayson's daughter, Sauda, testified that, on the night of Grayson's death, Grayson told her daughter that she was going out with [Jones]." *In re Jones*, 13 Cal.4th at 584. While it was also true that this evidence had been subject to some varying accounts and biases, the evidence came from several different sources and it can hardly be said that Jones has been shown to be "actually innocent."

The prosecution did not choose to drop charges because Jones was innocent. Rather, due to the passage of time, it no longer had the evidence and witnesses available to retry the case. *Modesto Bee*, (11/16/96); *Washington Times*, (9/12/99).

66. **Carl Lawson--***People v. Lawson*, 644 N.E.2d 1172 (Ill. 1994). Lawson was convicted of murdering eight year old Terrance Jones. The victim's body was found in an abandoned church. There was evidence that Lawson's romantic relationship with the young boy's mother had ended and that Lawson was upset about the breakup. Investigators discovered two bloody shoeprints of a commonly worn brand of gym shoe near the body. Lawson wore these type of shoes. The shoeprints were made near the time of the crime and were the only evidence capable of establishing Lawson's presence at the scene of the crime at the time it occurred. Various items were removed from around the victim's body. Two of the items near the body, a beer bottle and a matchbook, had Lawson's fingerprints. Lawson's first conviction was reversed because his attorney had a conflict of interest. He was acquitted at his second trial, apparently, because the shoeprint evidence could not be associated only with him–the shoe was too popular. However, this does not change the fact that Lawson's fingerprints were on items found near the body and that other evidence, albeit some of it highly inconsistent, remain to incriminate Lawson, including evidence of motive.

In addition, Lawson's case is an example of an intial conviction and death sentence reversed on appeal followed by an acquittal on retrial.

67. **David Wayne Grannis**– *Grannis v.* State, 900 P.2d 1 (Ariz. 1995). This recent addition to the DPIC List is not an example of an exoneration due to "actual innocence", but due to legally insufficient evidence to prove guilt beyond a reasonable doubt. Grannis and a co-defendant, Webster, were first tried and convicted together on the theory that they killed the victim while robbing him and burglarizing his house. Grannis's fingerprints were present at the scene. He testified at the trial and admitted that he was present at the victim's house. He claimed that the victim sexually attacked him and that Webster interceded. He was not present when Webster stabbed the victim to death. Their convictions were reversed because of the trial court erroneously admitted homosexual pornographic photos found in Grannis's closet. On remand, Grannis and Webster were tried separately. Webster was convicted and sentenced to death again. Although there was evidence that Grannis was with Webster when he bragged about the murder, that he and Webster were driving the victim's car, and that he destroyed

evidence, the trial court found insufficient evidence that Grannis had actually committed premeditated murder. *Ariz. Daily Star* (5/9/96, 11/7/96).

68. **Ricardo Aldape Guerra**--*Guerra v. Johnson*, 90 F.3d 1075 (5th Cir. 1996); *Guerra v. Collins*, 916 F.Supp. 620 (S.D.Tex. 1995); *Guerra v. State*, 771 S.W.2d 543 (Tex.Crim.App. 1988). Guerra was convicted as the triggerman, but evidence indicates he may have only been the accomplice. It is noted in the federal court opinion that Guerra was not prosecuted as an accomplice although he was undoubtedly present at the scene and in the company of the triggerman. He fled with the shooter from the scene and was hiding at the site of a subsequent shootout with the police. Near him was a gun wrapped in a bandanna. Originally, this factual distinction was not considered proof of "actual innocence". *Stanford*, at 43.

69. **Benjamin Harris**--*Harris (Ramseyer) v. Wood*, 64 F.3d 1432 (9th Cir. 1995). Harris was convicted of hiring a hit man named Bonds to murder a man named Turner. Harris gave numerous inconsistent statements about his whereabouts and involvement in the murder. Ultimately, Harris admitted taking turns with Bonds in shooting Turner, but denied hiring Bonds to shoot Turner. Harris did admit having a motive to murder Turner. He admitted driving the murderer Bonds to the scene and providing a gun. Initially, Harris confessed, but then testified at trial that he and Bonds took turns pulling the trigger.

By denying a contract killing, Harris hoped to avoid eligibility for the death penalty under Washington state law. A federal court vacated his conviction because of ineffective assistance of counsel. Although Harris's counsel claimed that Harris fantasized his confession, the prosecution chose not to retry Harris because the alleged hitman (Bonds) was in prison and would not testify, other witnesses were unavailable, and the federal court had ruled Harris's confession inadmissible.

Since Harris could not be retried, the prosecution sought his civil commitment based on a petition from hospital psychiatrists. He was confined in state a mental hospital, but a jury subsequently found he should be kept in a less restrictive environment. These circumstances do not support placing Harris on a list of the actually innocent. *Seattle Times*, (8/19/97,4/16/00); *Portland Oregonian*, (8/24/97); *Seattle Post-Intelligencer*, (7/17/97, 8/23/97); *Tacoma News Tribune*, (5/29/97).

70. **Robert Hayes**--*Hayes v. State*, 660 So.2d 257 (Fla. 1995). The initial conviction was based on a combination of DNA evidence, Hayes's inconsistent statements about when he was last with the victim, and hearsay statements by the victim expressing fear of Hayes. The Florida Supreme Court reversed the case because the trial court erroneously admitted DNA evidence matching Hayes with semen on the victim's shirt. The court held that a "band-shifting" technique used to identify the DNA had not reached the appropriate level of scientific acceptance–a Florida state opinion not universally shared. See, e.g. *State v. Copeland*, 922 P.2d 1304 (Wash. 1996). However, the court also held that the

trial court on retrial could consider admitting evidence of Hayes's semen in the victim's vagina. The appeals court opinion noted that "evidence exists in this case to establish that Hayes committed this offense, physical evidence also exists to establish that someone other than Hayes committed the offense."

On retrial, the trial court admitted evidence that Hayes' semen was in the victim's vagina. However, there was also evidence that the victim was clutching hairs in her hand inconsistent with Hayes' hair. The state attorney explained to the Florida Commission on Capital Cases: "In the end, the jury disregarded the fact that Hayes' DNA was found in the victim's vagina and acquitted of murder." Nothing about Hayes' retrial changes the appeals court's original observation that evidence existed to establish Hayes' guilt. The acquittal on retrial was based on reasonable doubt, not actual innocence.

71. **Randall Padgett**–*Padgett v. State*, 668 So.2d 78 (Ala. 1995). Padgett's conviction and sentence were reversed because the prosecution did not disclose some exculpatory blood testing evidence until in the middle of the trial and the trial court erroneously denied Padgett's motion for a mistrial. Padgett had been convicted of stabbing his estranged wife to death. He and his wife were separated. Padgett's wife knew Padgett was having an affair with their neighbor. The evidence showed that there was no forced entry into the house where Padgett's wife was living with their children. Nothing was stolen from the house, but it was undisputed that a sex act occurred with the victim at or near the time of her death. The day after the murder, Padgett left his children with an aunt and left town with his girlfriend without telling anyone or asking anyone to watch his children. A semen sample taken from the victim matched Padgett's DNA. Blood was also found at the scene that did not match the victim's. Although initial testing indicated the blood was consistent with Padgett's blood type, subsequent tests raised questions as to whether that blood sample was tainted or belonged to a third party. On retrial, it remained undisputed that Padgett's semen was found inside the victim. The victim had threatened to divorce Randall Padgett and he was in danger of losing his chicken farm. Padgett's defense on retrial was that "his lover killed his wife and put his semen in her." The girlfriend had threatened Padgett's wife. However, Padgett also claimed on retrial that his lover's motive to kill Padgett's wife was "to secure Randall Padgett." Although this motive does not explain why Padgett's lover would then frame Randall for the murder by placing his semen inside the victim and implicating him as the actual murderer, the jury acquitted Padgett on retrial. Under these circumstances, Padgett's acquittal does not establish "actual innocence". Padgett remains the "sole" suspect in the case. *Birmingham Post-Herald* (December, 2001).

72. **James "Bo" Cochran-** *Cochran v. Herring*, 43 F.3d 1404 (11th Cir. 1995); *Cochran v. State*, 500 So.2d 1161 (1984). This recent addition to the DPIC List is yet another example of an acquittal based on "reasonable doubt", rather than "actual innocence." *Birmingham Post-Herald* (December, 2001)

74. **Curtis Kyles**--*Kyles v. Whitley*, 514 U.S. 419 (1995). After one vacated conviction and four mistrials in which a jury was unable to reach a verdict over a 14-year period, the prosecutor chose not to retry Kyles although the final jury hung 8-4 for conviction (an earlier jury hung 10-2 for acquittal). The man whom Kyles alleged did the killing was himself killed by a member of Kyles' family in 1986. *New Orleans Times-Picayune*, (2/19/98,6/27/98); *Baton Rouge Advocate*, (2/19/98). A 5-4 United States Supreme Court split decision vacating Kyles' conviction due to prosecutorial misconduct disagreed on the strength of the evidence against Kyles. That disagreement itself certainly refutes any judgment that Kyles was actually innocent. Unfortunately, according to a recently published book on this case, it remains a "complicated and ambiguous case" in which prosecutorial misconduct may have "botch[ed]" the case and "framed the right man." Horne, *Desire Street* (2005).

75. **Shareef Cousin**--*State v. Cousin*, 710 So.2d 1065 (La. 1998). Contrary to the DPIC List's summary, Cousin's case was not reversed because of "improperly withheld evidence . . . ". In fact, the Louisiana Supreme Court explicitly did not rule on that issue. *State v. Cousin*, 710 So.2d at 1073 fn. 8. Rather, the Louisiana high court reversed Cousin's conviction because the prosecutor improperly impeached a witness with prior inconsistent statements recounting a confession made to him by Cousin. In other words, to prove the case against Cousin, the prosecutor brought out the fact that the witness had previously told the police that Cousin had confessed to the crime. Under Louisiana law, such prior statements cannot be used as substantive evidence of the defendant"s guilt. *State v. Brown*, 674 So.2d 428 (La.App. 1996) Other jurisdictions, of course, would not necessarily find this evidence inadmissible as substantive evidence. See *State v. Owunta*, 761 So.2d 528 (La. 2000) (acknowledging that Louisiana follows the minority rule in not allowing prior inconsistent statements to be used as substantive evidence). Thus, Cousin's conviction may have been upheld in other states. See *California v. Green*, 399 U.S. 49 (1970). Without these statements, the prosecution determined that the remaining evidence (weak or tentative identifications and Cousin's incriminating comment that the arrest warrant had the wrong date for the murder) was insufficient to carry the burden of proof. *Baton Rouge Saturday State Times/Morning Advocate* (1/9/99); *New Orleans Times-Picayune* (1/9/99). Cousin was not retried because the prosecution believed he was "actually innocent," but because Louisiana state law precluded evidence of guilt in this case that would actually have been admissible in other states.

77. **Steven Smith**– *People v. Smith*, 565 N.E.2d 900 (Ill. 1991); *People v. Smith*, 708 N.E.2d 365 (Ill. 1999). In this case, Smith was accused of assassinating an assistant prison warden while the victim was standing by his car in a local bar's parking lot. Various witnesses testified that they saw Smith and two other men in the bar and then departing just before the victim left.

The prosecution's theory was that Smith murdered the victim at the behest of a local neighborhood criminal gang leader. One eyewitness, who knew Smith, identified him as the shooter. When Smith was arrested, he was talking to the leader of the local gang. There was testimony that on certain occasions, Smith had been seen in the company of the gang leader. When the police searched Smith's residence they seized 77 pages of documents including regulations or bylaws of the criminal gang , other information relating to the gang, and two invitations to recent gang functions. However, at trial, the court excluded this evidence of Smith's association with the gang. The trial court admitted evidence of gang-related activity in the Illinois prison system, that the victim was a strict disciplinarian, and that the leader of Smith's gang had had an altercation with the victim. However, the trial court excluded the evidence seized in Smith's residence connecting him to the prison gang. On appeal, Smith's conviction was reversed because there was no evidence at trial connecting Smith to the prison gang! The irony was not lost on the dissenting judge: "If there was error at trial, it occurred not because the trial judge admitted too much evidence, but because he admitted too little."

Smith's conviction after retrial was then reversed for insufficient evidence. In any event, although various witnesses identified Smith in the bar before the victim was shot, only one eyewitness identified Smith as the actual shooter. The appellate court found that there were too many serious inconsistencies and impeachment of that witness at the trial to support Smith's conviction for shooting the victim. The court rejected the State's arguments reconciling some of the conflicting accounts of the shooting, although only because the State had not raised these arguments until it was too late for the defense to challenge the State's theory. It is not clear if the witness was confronted with previous statements that were consistent with the accounts of other witnesses. Ordinarily, the testimony of a single witness is sufficient to convict. However, the Illinois court explained that the conviction may be rejected if the witnesses' testimony "is so unreasonable, improbable, or unsatisfactory as to justify a reasonable doubt of defendant's guilt." At best, the circumstantial evidence "tending to link defendant to the murder merely narrowed the class of individuals who may have killed the victim...." Given the evidence, Smith appears to have been an accomplice to the shooting even if he was not the actual triggerman. He was certainly not eliminated from the "class of individuals who may have killed the victim....".

Significantly, in reversing Smith's conviction and ending any chance for another retrial, the appellate court explained: "While a not guilty finding is sometimes equated with a finding of innocence, that conclusion is erroneous. Courts do not find people guilty or innocent. They find them guilty or not guilty. A not guilty verdict expresses no view as to a defendant's innocence. Rather, it indicates simply that the prosecution has failed to meet its burden of proof. While there are those who may criticize courts for turning criminals loose, courts have a duty to ensure that all citizens receive those rights which are applicable equally to every citizen who may find himself charged with a crime, whatever the crime and whatever the circumstances. When the State cannot meet its burden of proof, the defendant must go free. This case happens to be a murder case carrying a sentence of death against a defendant where the State has failed to meet its burden. It is no help to speculate that the defendant may have killed the victim." In short, as the appeals court took pains to emphasize, the evidence against Smith was legally insufficient, but it was not shown that he was "actually innocent".

78. **Ronald Keith Williamson-** Even widely touted DNA exonerations are sometimes less than they seem. For instance, the recent decision by the Oklahoma authorities not to retry Williamson after DNA testing established that the victim's body did not contain his semen did not automatically make him "poster material for Actual Innocence".

Recent Congressional testimony by the Oklahoma Attorney General indicates there is more to this story:

"Last Sunday's Tulsa World had a review of the book *Actual Innocence* which included a lengthy reference to the Oklahoma case of Ronald Keith Williamson, declared by the authors to have been proven innocent beyond a doubt after having been within days of being executed. It is a fact that Williamson was released on the strength of DNA testing, which showed that samples taken from the victim belonged to a third individual and not to Williamson or his co-defendant Dennis Fritz, who was also released from a life sentence. It is not true that Williamson was within days of being executed and it is arguable whether he is innocent.

"Oklahoma requested an execution date for Williamson in August 1994 because his most recent appeal had been denied and his next appeal had not been filed. An execution date of September 27, 1994 was set with all parties understanding that it could be stayed when the defense filed its petition for writ of habeas corpus, the next step in the process. The habeas petition was filed on September 22, 1994 and we filed a response agreeing to a stay of execution, which was granted September 23, 1994. The threat of his execution on September 27 was so remote as to be nonexistent.

"Williamson was not convicted 'on the strength of a jailhouse snitch' as reported. Among the direct and circumstantial evidence of his guilt was a statement he gave to the Oklahoma State Bureau of Investigation describing a "dream" in which he had committed the murder. Williamson said, "I was on her, had a cord around her neck, stabbed her frequently, pulled the rope tight around her neck." He paused and then stated that he was worried about what this would do to his family.

"When asked if Fritz was there, Williamson said, 'yes.'

> **"When asked if he went there with the intention of killing her, Williamson said 'probably'**
>
> **"In response to the question of why he killed her, Williamson said, 'she made me mad.'**

"The Pontotoc County prosecutor had a tough decision to make on a re-prosecution of Williamson and Fritz and concluded that conviction was highly unlikely in the wake of the DNA evidence, even though the note left at the scene said "Don't look fore us or ealse," [sic] indicating multiple perpetrators.

"Scheck, Neufeld, and Dwyer can claim Williamson as poster material for *Actual Innocence*, but I would look further before creating federal legislation based upon his case."

Testimony of the Honorable W.A. Drew Edmondson, Attorney General of the State of Oklahoma, Senate Judiciary Committee, 6/13/00.

Although Williamson suffered from mental problems that included delusional thinking, there was nothing presented to indicate that he would coincidentally "imagine" the actual facts of the murder. The victim had small puncture wounds and cuts. There was a semicircular ligature mark on her neck. The cause of death was suffocation due to a washcloth in her mouth and the ligature tightened around her neck. Thus, Williamson's "dream" was consistent with the murder. Given the evidence of Williamson's alleged mental problems, there is no more reason to believe his denials of guilt than his incriminating statements.

Furthermore, the DNA testing showed only that the semen in the victim's body belonged to another man named Gore. However, as the Attorney General's statement indicates, the evidence at trial indicated that more than one person could have been involved in the assault on the victim. The evidence of a group involvement in the murderous assault means that the failure to find Williamson's semen in the victim does not eliminate him as a participant in her assault. He may be exonerated as a perpetrator of the sexual assault, but he is not necessarily exonerated as an accomplice. Compare *People v. Gholston* (Ill.App. 1998) 697 N.E.2d 415; *Mebane v. State* (Kan.App. 1995) 902 P.2d 494; Note, 62 *Ohio L.J.* 1195, 1241 fn.46; Nat'l Comm'n on the Future of DNA Evidence, Post Conviction Testing: Recommendations for Handling Requests, September 1999; NIJ Research Report, Convicted by Juries, Exonerated by Science: Case Studies in the Use of DNA Evidence to Establish Innocence After Trial, June 1996 (all discussing potentially inconclusive DNA results in cases involving multiple defendants).

80. **Clarence Richard Dexter**-- *State v. Dexter*, 954 S.W.2d 332 (1997). The conviction and death sentence were reversed for prosecutorial misconduct at trial. Dexter could not be retried because of lost evidence. *Tulsa World* (4/23/99,6/5/99, 6/8/99, 6/9/99, 6/11/99, 12/29/99).

81. **Warren Douglas Manning**-- *State v. Manning*, 409 S.E.2d 372 (S.C. 1991); *State v. Manning*, 495 S.E.2d 191 (S.C. 1997). There were five trials in this case, including two convictions that were reversed and two mistrials, before Manning was acquitted.

Manning was convicted of murdering a state trooper who had taken him into custody for driving with a suspended license. Manning first stated that the victim had released him with a warning ticket, but then explained that he escaped from the trooper's car when the trooper stopped another car. However, the trooper was shot with his own revolver and that revolver was seized in a barn behind Manning's residence. Other circumstantial evidence was also consistent with Manning's guilt. Manning was acquitted in his fifth trial based on a defense of reasonable doubt. Hence, his defense lawyer conceded in argument to the jury that "[i]f there wasn't any case against Warren Manning, then we wouldn't be here. But the law requires that the state prove him guilty beyond a reasonable doubt. Without that, the law says you cannot find him guilty." *Associated Press*, 9/30/99. Manning's acquittal on retrial does not mean that Manning was "actually innocent."

The two reversals of Manning's two convictions and death sentences were based on instructional and change of venue issues. The properly tried retrial ultimately resulted in his acquittal. Due to the errors in the first trials, Manning's inclusion on the DPIC List because of his acquittal does little to advance the argument about the potential hazards of sentencing the innocent to death in the American criminal justice system.

82. **Alfred Rivera**– *State v. Rivera*, 514 S.E.2d 720 (N.C. 1999). Rivera's conviction and death sentence were reversed because the trial court made an evidentiary error in excluding evidence that Rivera may have been "framed". Additional prosecutorial misconduct in argument and instructional error occurred at the trial as well. On retrial, Rivera was acquitted despite some conflicting evidence. According to a juror, the jury believed there was a reasonable doubt about Rivera's guilt. Rivera's release is another example of an acquittal following the appellate correction of a trial court evidentiary hearing. It is speculative that Rivera would have been sentenced to death at all but for the "trial errors" at the first trial.

83. **Steve Manning**-- *People v. Manning*, 695 N.E.2d 423 (Ill. 1998). The prosecution exercised its discretion not to retry Manning after his conviction was reversed. The Illinois Supreme Court forbade the use of certain evidence including questionable informant testimony. However, the Illinois Supreme Court also excluded the victim's wife's hearsay testimony that the victim had warned her that if he was ever killed to tell the FBI that Manning killed him. Apparently, the victim had told his wife that Manning had "ripped him off for a lot of money "and he was going to get the money back. Thus, while legally inadmissible under state law, there was evidence that Manning had a motive to murder the victim. It was also "consolation" to the district attorney in not retrying the case that Manning, a former cop gone bad, was already serving two life sentences plus 100 years for kidnaping in Missouri. *Chicago Tribune*, 1/19/00. Manning's case, of course, is also another example of where it is speculative whether the defendant would have been convicted and sentenced to Death Row if "trial errors" had not occurred at his first trial. "Steven Manning is another case in which it appears the system worked." 86 *Judicature* 83, 88 (September-October 2002).

85. **Joseph N. Green, Jr.**--*Green v. State,* 688 So.2d 301 (Fla. 1997). The prosecution's case in this robbery-murder was based on the victim's dying declaration, an eyewitness, and "circumstantial evidence that Green had the opportunity to kill" the victim. Green's conviction and death sentence were reversed because the prosecution improperly cross-examined a defense witness and because the trial court erroneously denied a suppression motion. On retrial, the critical eyewitness was found incompetent to testify. This eyewitness had given inconsistent and contradictory testimony. The trial court then dismissed the case because there was no physical evidence connecting Green to the murder. The trial court found that there was a reasonable doubt about Green's guilt and it was "possible" someone else had committed the crime. However, the victim's dying declaration describing her assailant was generally consistent with Green's description, i.e., a slim black man in his mid-20's. The victim also said the murderer fled toward the motel where Green resided. Green needed money. Furthermore, when Green was arrested, he gave inconsistent statements about his activities on the night of the murder although one of his alibis did receive some corroboration. *St. Petersburg Times* (12/29/99, 3/17/00.) Thus, while there may not be sufficient evidence of Green's guilt, the evidence hardly establishes his innocence.

The recent report of the Florida Commission on Capital Cases sheds additional information on this case. Prior to the first trial, the court suppressed evidence of gun power residue in the pockets of Green's clothing. Although the trial court had originally found the eyewitness competent to testify at the first trial, it reversed itself on retrial and found the witness incompetent. The prosecution reiterated that Green had "been given the benefit of the doubt", but that his innocence was not established since he had motive, opportunity, and problems with his alibi. Green's defense attorney actually attributed his client's acquittal at least partially to the "bad search warrant" served in the case. Since the search warrant was "bad", evidence of Green's guilt such as the gun residue in his pocket was never presented to the jury.

87. **William Nieves** -- *Commonwealth v. Nieves,* 746 A.2d 1102 (Pa. 2000). This Hispanic defendant was convicted of murdering Eric McAiley due to a drug debt. As the police sped to the scene of the murder, a bearded Hispanic in a Cadillac pointed out where the murder occurred and drove away. A witness ultimately identified Nieves as the man who got out of a Cadillac and shot McAiley. The witness also admitted that she initially failed to identify Nieves. McAiley's nephew testified that McAiley sold drugs for Nieves. Another witness testified that before the murder he overheard Nieves warn McAiley, "Better get me my fucking money, I'm not playing with you." Nieves did not testify at the guilt phase of his first trial because his lawyer erroneously advised him that he would be impeached with his prior record of firearms and drug trafficking offenses. Ultimately, Nieves did testify at his penalty phase. He admitted he was a "small-time drug dealer" who had only a few drug transactions with McAiley. Nieves' case was reversed because of his attorney's faulty advice about whether he would be impeached if he testified.

Nieves was acquitted on retrial. His retrial defense again impeached the eyewitness who identified Nieves with prior conflicting statements she had made, including that she had initially identified two thin black men and then a husky Hispanic. The witness denied identifying the assailant(s) as black men. Nieves is Hispanic, but not "husky." Another witness testified that he saw a black man shoot McAiley, but this witness' testimony was also rife with inconsistencies. The Philadelphia district attorney continues to maintain that Nieves is guilty. The Nieves case is not an example of a defendant who was found actually innocent, but of a defendant for which the prosecution could not prove guilt beyond a reasonable doubt. *Associated Press* (10/20/00, 5/14/01, 5/25/01).

89. **Michael Graham &**

90. **Ronnie Burrell**--The Louisiana Attorney General dismissed charges rather than retrying these two defendants after their convictions were vacated due to a witness recantation and the discovery of significant impeaching evidence of a jailhouse informant. The Louisiana Attorney General's decision was not based on "innocence," but on the lack of sufficient credible evidence to establish guilt. However, Graham's and Burrell's own counsel acknowledge that new evidence could result in reinstatement of the charges and they have instructed their clients not to discuss the case. Contrary to the DPIC summary, DNA played no role in this case. The case was not dismissed because Graham and Burrell have been established as "innocent," only because there was insufficient evidence of guilt. *Baton Rouge Advocate* (3/20/01, 3/21/01, 3/30/02); *Minneapolis-St. Paul Star Tribune* (1/1/01).

91. **Oscar Lee Morris**- *People v. Morris*, 46 Cal.3d 1 (Cal. 1988); *People v. Oscar Lee Morris* (BH001152) (order dated 1/21/00). Morris's death sentence was reversed on appeal because there was insufficient evidence he was eligible for the death penalty. Accordingly, he was resentenced to life imprisonment without the possibility of parole. Morris was subsequently released on habeas corpus when the principal witness in his case provided a deathbed recantation to Morris's counsel. The trial court found the recantation to be a reliable declaration against penal interest since it was corroborated by the testimony of the dead witnesses's girlfriend and cousin. However, the trial court also noted that the recantation occurred under "suspicious circumstances" and was not supported by a polygraph examination administered by Morris's advocates. Without the dead witness, the only remaining evidence of Morris's guilt was testimony that he resembled the murderer and attempted to use the murder victim's credit card three days after the murder. He also had access to an auto similar to one driven by the murderer. The recantation sufficiently undermined the case to justify a new trial. Under these circumstances, the Los Angeles County district attorney was unable to retry Morris. After his release, Morris unsuccessfully sued the city for violation of his civil rights relating to concealment of benefits to the dead witness. The city's attorney referred to the recantation as "an under-the-cover recitation with nobody who can verify it one way or another." *San Francisco Daily Journal*, 10/29/02; *Long Beach Press Telegram*, 11/21/02;

92. **Peter Limone** -- *Limone v. Massachusetts,* 408 U.S. 936 (1972). As with Lawyer Johnson, Limone was convicted and sentenced under Massachusetts' defunct, pre-1976 death penalty statute.

93. **Gary Drinkard**–*Ex parte Drinkard*, 777 S.2d 295 (ala. 2000); *Drinkard v. State*, 777 S.2d 1998 (Ala.Crim.App. 1999). Drinkard was acquitted on retrial after his conviction was reversed on review on state appellate review by the Alabama Supreme Court because the prosecution had introduced evidence that Drinkard committed an unrelated burglary. Thus, this case is no more than another example of the conventional appellate system working to correct a trial error. *Birmingham Post* (December, 2001).

94. **Joaquin Martinez**-- *Martinez v. State*, 261 So.2d 1074 (Fla. 2000). Spanish native Martinez was accused of murdering a couple at their home sometime between October 27, 1995 and October 30, 1995. One victim was shot and the other victim died of multiple stab wounds. There was no physical evidence of a forced entry, indicating that the victims knew their assailant. A phone list in the kitchen included a pager number for "Joe." After the police left several messages for "Joe," Martinez's ex-wife, Sloane, called and explained she had the pager. She advised the police of her suspicions that Martinez was involved in the murders. The detective listened to a phone conversation Martinez had with his ex-wife in which he stated, "[T]his is something that I explained to you before, and that I am going to get the death penalty for what I did." When she asked him if he was referring to the murder, he cryptically replied, "No, I can't talk to you about it on the phone right now." Martinez's ex-wife Sloane then had a surreptitiously recorded conversation at her home during which Martinez made "several remarks that could be interpreted as incriminating." Martinez's girlfriend testified that Martinez went out on October 27 and returned with ill-fitting clothes, a swollen lip, and scraped knuckles. Another witness testified he saw Martinez on October 27 and that he looked like he had been in a fight. Three inmates testified to incriminating statements by Martinez. The prosecution relied primarily on Sloane's testimony and the surreptitious tape. Sloane testified about the contents of the taped conversations, Martinez's behavior, and other statements he had made to her as well.

Martinez's case was reversed because a police witness erroneously testified as to his opinion that Martinez was guilty. The case was returned for retrial and the prosecution suffered many of the problems that occur on retrial in terms of changes in the evidence. Due to the passage of time, a witness had died, another witness had refused to cooperate (apparently Martinez's girlfriend), and the third witness (Martinez's ex-wife Sloane) had recanted.

Furthermore, a major piece of prosecution evidence was excluded on retrial. At Martinez's first trial, the trial court overruled Martinez's objection that the incriminating tape of his conversation with ex-wife Sloane was unintelligible and incomplete. The trial court allowed the tape to be played while the jury read a transcript. On appeal, Martinez did not challenge the admission of the tape. However, several of the judges on the appeals court noted that the tape was of "poor quality and portions of the conversation are difficult to hear . . . " However, one concurring justice specifically stated that the tape recording was "sufficiently audible to be admitted . . . " In any event, even if portions of the tape were inaudible, Sloane Martinez could herself testify as to what was said during her incriminating conversation with Martinez. There seems to be no question that Martinez made potentially incriminating statements on the tape.

Nevertheless, on retrial and despite the appeals court indications that portions of the tape were audible , the trial court excluded the tape completely as inaudible.[28] Sloane Martinez now stated that she had lied about what her former husband had said. The tape was not available to contradict her. The prosecution chose not to call Sloane to testify and instead relied on a police officer to testify from memory about what he had heard when Martinez's incriminating conversation with Sloane. However, the officer had no independent recollection any more of the conversation and had to rely on a transcript of the recording. The jury's request to hear the actual tape was denied. *Associated Press*(6/6/01); *St. Petersburg Times* (6/7/01). Martinez's acquittal on retrial appears attributable to a deterioration and gutting of the prosecution's evidence, not proof of innocence. Both the prosecution and the defense advised the Florida Commission on Capital Cases that the prosecution was unable to present the same evidence at Martinez's retrial.

95. **Jeremy Sheets**-- *State v. Sheets*, 618 N.W.2d 117 (Neb. 2000); *Sheets v. Butera*, 389 F.3d 772 (8th Cir. 2004). The appellate court decision explains that Sheets was convicted of a racially motivated murder of a young African American girl. The evidence of Sheets' guilt included the tape-recorded statements of an accomplice named Barnett, who had died prior to Sheets' trial. The Nebraska Supreme Court reversed the conviction because Sheets could not cross-examine the dead accomplice.

According to newspaper accounts, the prosecutor did not retry the case since he believed there was insufficient evidence to convict Sheets beyond a reasonable doubt, not because the prosecutor believed that Sheets was innocent. In fact, Sheets' arrest originally resulted from a tip based on Barnett's statements that he and Sheets had murdered the victim. The tipster then tape recorded statements by Barnett implicating Sheets as the murderer. Once again, there is no reason to doubt the reliability of this particular taped statement by Barnett since it occurred before Barnett's arrest. Sheets' own testimony that he did not buy a car involved in the murder until after the murder occurred was contradicted by other police testimony. Testimony was also presented that Sheets had threatened an African American neighbor and had a fascination with Nazism, including shaving his head and drawing swastikas.

Most significantly, Sheets later requested a refund of the monies deposited in the Victim's Compensation Fund on his behalf. The Nebraska Attorney General pointed out in denying Sheets' request that the reversal of Sheets' conviction is not even considered a "disposition of charges favorable" to the defendant unless the case is subsequently dismissed because the prosecution is convinced that the accused is innocent. Neb. Op. Atty. Gen. No. 01036; Omaha World Herald, 5/6/97, 6/13/01. Since the dismissal was not on the basis of innocence, Sheets' request for compensation was denied.

The Eighth Circuit Court of Appeals has also rejected Sheets' civil rights suit against the investigating officers relating to the circumstances of Barnett's statements. The court found no evidence that the police overcame Barnett's free will and impaired his capacity to make the statements implicating himself and Sheets in the murder. There was no indication the police "fed" information about the crime to Barnett.

97. **Juan Roberto Melendez**--*Melendez v. State*, 498 So.2d 1258 (Fla. 1986); *Melendez v. State*, 612 So.2d 1366 (Fla. 1992); *Melendez v. Singletary*, 644 So.2d 983 (Fla. 1994); *Melendez v. State*, 718 So.2d 746 (Fla. 1998). Melendez was convicted of murdering a beauty salon owner in 1984. Melendez's conviction was based on the testimony of a friend John Berrien and of a David Falcon, who claimed Melendez confessed to him in jail. The defense relied on alibi and presented evidence that a third party named James had confessed to murdering the victim. The defense also impeached Falcon as a paid informant.

After his conviction, Melendez continued to attack the credibility of the prosecution's witnesses and to further support his defense that James actually committed the murder. Various witnesses testified as to incriminating statements by James. However, James never explicitly confessed to these witnesses or he otherwise gave conflicting explanations for murdering the victim. His accounts of the murder also conflicted. Berrien partially recanted and it was revealed he had negotiated a deal for his testimony. However, none of these witnesses who provided this new information for Melendez were found to be credible.

Then, Melendez's original trial attorney suddenly discovered a long-forgotten transcript of a jailhouse confession by James. It was not explained why this transcript had not been used at trial. Apparently, according to this transcript, James had also confessed to a state investigator. The suddenly discovered transcript and the Berrien recantation coupled with the belated revelation of a deal for his testimony were sufficient for a court to order a new trial. However, by this time, James and Falcon were both dead. Thus, there was no longer any opportunity for the prosecution to explore and impeach their conflicting accounts. On that basis, although the prosecution continued to believe that Melendez was the murderer, the prosecution decided there was insufficient evidence for a new trial and dismissed the case. *Sun Herald*, 1/6/02;*The Guardian*, 1/5/02; *St. Petersburg Times*, 1/4/02, 1/5/02; *Tampa Tribune*, 1/3/02; 1/4/02.

98. **Ray Krone**–*State v. Krone*, 897 P.2d 621 (Ariz. 1995). Although Krone was cleared by DNA evidence, he was not on Death Row when he was released. His first conviction

and death sentence had been reversed because the trial court denied a continuance when the prosecution failed to provide timely discovery. He was sentenced to life on retrial.

99. **Thomas H. Kimbell**- *Commonwealth v. Kimbell*, 759 A.2d 256 (Pa. 2000). Kimbell's acquittal on retrial is another example of a case in which the prosecution could not prove guilt beyond a reasonable doubt, but the acquittal did not establish Kimbell's innocence.

Kimbell's defense at his first trial was that another member of the victim's family, probably the husband, committed the murder. The victim's mother had testified that she had been talking on the telephone with her daughter shortly before the murders (between two and three in the afternoon) when her daughter said she had to go because "someone" had pulled into the driveway (possibly the murderer). Previously, the mother had told the police that her daughter had said that her husband had driven into the driveway. The Pennsylvania Supreme Court reversed Kimbell's conviction because Kimbell's lawyer was not allowed to impeach the mother with her prior inconsistent statement that her daughter had specifically said that her husband (not just "someone") was arriving at the house. The court agreed that this testimony could have created a reasonable doubt about Kimbell's guilt.

Despite the acquittal on retrial, the prosecution maintained that Kimbell was the murderer and noted that "the more time that elapses between a crime and a trial, the harder it can be to obtain a conviction." Lost in the shuffle was evidence casting doubt on the credibility of the mother's testimony and recollection in general, given her understandable grief about her daughter's murder. At the first trial, a psychiatrist had testified that the mother's testimony "could be affected by the impact that the slayings have had on her." Indeed, when the mother testified at the first trial, she repeatedly broke down sobbing and said she had talked to her daughter a "whole bunch" and that the conversations were "mixed up together". She had also told investigators before that her daughter had hung up to make dinner, but she could not remember that previous statement. Furthermore, another witness had testified that he did stop briefly at the victims' home at around 2:00 p.m. to make a phone call and then left (although this person could have been the person whom the daughter referred to in the phone call with her mother, he is apparently not considered a suspect in the case). When Kimbell was interviewed by the police he provided them information about the murder that he claimed he overheard on police scanners, but this information had not been broadcast on the police radios.

At the first trial, a friend of Kimbell's testified that Kimbell had pointed at the victims' home after the murders and admitted killing the people. However, this witness died after the first trial. Other witnesses had identified Kimbell as being near the victims' home on the day of the murder and other witnesses had testified to incriminating admissions by Kimbell. *Pittsburgh Post-Gazette*, 5/4/02; 5/6/98, 5/2/98; 2/4/97; *Associated Press*, 5/6/98.

While there might have been "reasonable doubt" about Kimbell's guilt, the available information does not exonerate him. "But the reality is that we don't know for sure why the two Kimbell juries came to two different conclusions." Kurtis, *The Death Penalty on Trial* (2004) at p. 195. Also, as with many of the cases on the DPIC List, Kimbell's case is an example of an acquittal following a reversal based on "trial error", it is speculative whether he would have been sent to Death Row at all if error had not occurred at the first trial.

100. **Larry Osborne**--*Osborne v. Commonwealth,* 43 S.W.3d 234 (Ky.2001). Osborne was convicted of breaking into the home of an elderly couple, bludgeoning them, and burning their house down. Osborne was acquitted on retrial due to reasonable doubt, but not because the evidence established that he was not the actual culprit. A friend and potential accomplice of Osborne's implicated Osborne in a grand jury proceeding. However, this witness then died by drowning before the first trial. Instead, his grand jury testimony was read at Osborne's first trial. The conviction was reversed because of the admission of the dead witnesses' grand jury testimony–since there was no opportunity for Osborne to cross-examine the witness. On retrial, without the grand jury testimony of the dead witness, the prosecution had insufficient evidence to convince the jury of Osborne's guilt beyond a reasonable doubt. Nevertheless, there was evidence that Osborne and his mother staged a phony "911" call to the police in order to divert police attention to another potential perpetrator. There was also a dispute whether Osborne possessed a set of wire cutters removed from the victims' home. *Louisville Courier-Journal* (8/2/02; 8/3/02); *Associated Press* (8/2/02). Osborne's case is also another example of a defendant who might not have gone to Death Row at all but for "trial court" error at the first trial.

105. **Rudolph Holton**-- *Holton v. State.* 573 So.2d 284 (Fla. 1991). Rather than a case of "actual innocence", Holton's case is the an example of a decision by the prosecution that it no longer had sufficient evidence to prove guilt beyond a reasonable doubt. This case's inclusion on the DPIC List is another example of the misleading inadequacy of its criteria.

Holton was convicted of raping and strangling a woman in an abandoned building, then setting the building on fire. Holton initially denied being in the house, until he was confronted with a cigarette pack with his fingerprints recovered at the crime scene. Based on scientific evidence, the prosecution argued that the victim had several of Holton's hairs in her mouth. Witnesses against Holton included an individual who claimed to see a man who resembled Holton at the scene, another witness who claimed Holton admitted the murder, and another witness who claimed to see Holton talking to the victim outside the house before the fire.

Claims that Holton was exonerated because of DNA and recanting witnesses have been greatly exaggerated. The decision of the trial court granting Holton post-conviction relief is based on the prosecution's failure to disclose evidence that the victim had reported a rape at the same address ten days before and evidence of consideration received by one of the witnesses. There was also evidence from a witness who suddenly stepped forward for the first time that suggested that the person who previously raped the victim confessed to her murder. (However, the potential other suspect has denied involvement in the murder and voluntarily submitted to a DNA test.) In addition, DNA showed that the hair in the victim's mouth was the victim's, not Holton's. However, the trial court rejected Holton's claims of newly-discovered evidence. In particular, when two witnesses recanted, the trial court found both of those recantations "unpersuasive". (Subsequently, both of these witnesses recanted their recantations.) The court also found "unpersuasive" evidence that scratch marks found on Holton's face were not "fresh". However, the court did find that the DNA evidence that the hairs in the victim's mouth were hers, not Holton's, was "of such a nature that it would probably produce an acquittal on retrial or result in a life sentence, rather than a death penalty." *State v. Holton*, Order denying in Part, and Granting, in Part Defendant's Motion to Vacate Judgment and Sentence with Special Requst for Leave to Amend, Case Nos. 86-08931 & 86-15176 (f.11/2/01)

(posted on http://www.oranous.com/innocence/RudolphHolton/innocent.html .)

When the Florida Supreme Court denied the prosecution's appeal, the prosecution made the practical decision that the lack of hair evidence coupled with the inconsistent testimony of the witnesses (despite the unpersuasive recantations) and the potential other suspect made it improbable that Holton or anyone could be convicted. Other witnesses had died and no other physical evidence connected Holton to the crime. The prosecutor explained: "I am not saying loud and clear that Rudolph Holton is innocent. I am saying we cannot prove his guilt beyond a reasonable doubt." . *Los Angeles Times* (1/25/03); *Tampa Tribune* (1/25/03, 11/3/01); *St. Petersburg Times* (4/24/01,11/3/01).

106. **Lemuel Prion**-*State v. Prion*, 52 P.3d 189 (Ariz. 2002). The Arizona Supreme Court reversed Prion's conviction and the Arizona prosecutor chose not to retry him. However, the decision not to retry Prion was not based on considerations of "actual innocence", but because of the prosecutor's decision that there was not enough evidence for a jury to find Prior guilty beyond a reasonable doubt. "Prosecutors decided Prion most likely would have been acquitted if prosecuted under the limits set by the [Arizona Supreme Court] ruling." The prosecution indicated it would "reopen the investigation and may refile charges." In this case, the victim's severed arms were recovered from a dumpster. The bones were cut by a heavy knife. Prion owned several knives, including a machete, and had been to a location near the dumpster where the victim's arms were recovered. He admitted to a fellow employee that he was afraid he would kill someone. He habitually talked about committing violent acts on women and admitting thinking about threatening a woman with his machete. He thought a picture of the victim was familiar, but he also thought he would have recalled her large chest. A "weak" identification placed Prion with the victim the night she disappeared. However, there was also evidence of another suspect who was connected with the victim the night she disappeared, had lied to the police, and had a history sexual violence. Due to the Arizona

Supreme Court's ruling, the prosecution would have been prohibited from introducing evidence of an unrelated sexual attack committed by Prion and the defense would have been allowed to introduce evidence of the alternative suspect. Under these circumstances, '[p]rosecutors decided Prion most likely would have been acquitted if prosecuted under the limits set by the [Arizona Supreme Court] ruling." *Tucson Citizen* (3/15/03).

107. **Wesley Quick**-*Quick v. State*, 825 S.2d 246 (Ala.App. 2001). After a mistrial, Quick was convicted of the multiple murder of two boys. He testified he was on LSD and did not remember what had happened, although he recalled driving away from the scene. The Alabama Court of Criminal Appeals reversed the judgment because the trial court erroneously denied Quick's attempts to impeach witnesses with his recollection of their inconsistent testimony at his first trial and because the trial court denied Quick a transcript of the original trial. The court noted that this transcript was necessary to impeach critical witnesses. Quick was acquitted on retrial even though he testified that he was present when another person killed the boys and threatened to kill someone else if Quick implicated him. Although Quick claimed he was too scarred to implicate the other culprit at the earlier trial, he did so at this subsequent trial. Due to the state court review, Quick was able to impeach witnesses with their prior testimony, something he had been erroneously prevented from doing at the earlier trial. This case is not an example of an exoneration by acquittal, but rather an example of the state process correcting trial error for retrial.

109. **Timothy Howard**

110. **Gary Lamar Jones**–These two recent additions to the DPIC List were both sentenced under Ohio's unconstitutional death penalty statute in 1976. Their sentences were automatically reduced to life in 1978.

114. **Gordon "Randy" Steidl**- *People v. Steidl,* 685 N.E.2d 1335 (1997).This defendant is another example of an inmate who had already been removed from Death Row due to the state post-conviction review process. The Illinois Supreme Court ordered an evidentiary hearing in Steidl's case which resulted in a new sentencing hearing in which he was resentenced to a life term.

115. **Laurence Adams**-This very recent addition to the DPIC List is also irrelevant to any assessment of wrongful convictions under a constitutional system of capital punishment. He was originally sentenced to death under Massachusetts' unconstitutional death penalty statute and his sentence was reduced to life.

116. **Dan L. Bright** - *State v. Bright,* 776 S.2d 1134 (La. 2000). This defendant's death sentence had already been vacated when the Louisiana Supreme Court found insufficient evidence of first degree murder and reduced his conviction to second degree murder.

117. **Ryan Matthews**- This defendant was sentenced to death for a murder that occurred when he was under 18 years of age. Under current law, he would no longer be eligible for the death penalty because he was a juvenile at the time of the crime.

119. **Derrick Jamison**-*Jamison v. Collins*, 291 F.3d 380 (6th Cir. 2002). The judgment in the most recent addition to the DPIC List was reversed because the prosecution failed to disclose evidence favorable to the defense, including evidence that could have impeached the testimony of the State's principal witness. The prosecution dropped efforts to retry the case due to evidentiary issues caused by the passage of time. Several witnesses had died or were unavailable.. The principal witness had been hard to find and when he was found, he claimed that he could no longer remember what happened due to intervening alcohol problems. The prosecution could not read transcripts of the witnesses' prior testimony into the record. *Associated Press* (3/1/05); *Cincinnati Post*, (1/03/04, 2/28/05, 3/1/05).

.

IMPLICATIONS AND CONCLUSION

"[T]he argument that innocent people may be executed-in small or large numbers-is not new; it has been central to the centuries-old debate over both the wisdom and the constitutionality of capital punishment...." *United States v. Quinones*, 313 F.3d 49, 63 (2nd Cir. 2002)[hereafter *Quinones II]* reversing *United States v. Quinones*, 205 F.Supp.2d 256 (N.Y.S.D. 2002) cert. den. *Quninones v. United States*, 540 U.S. 1051 (2003). There has always been a "recognition of the possibility that, because our judicial system–indeed, any judicial system–is fallible, innocent people might be executed and, therefore, lose any opportunity for exoneration." *Quinones*,, 313 F.3d at 64-65. This risk was recognized by the United States Supreme Court in *Furman v. Georgia*, 408 U.S. 238 (1972). *Quinones II*, at 65-67. Yet after *Furman* and despite that risk, 35 states enacted death penalty statutes. *Gregg v.Georgia*, 428 U.S. 153, 180 (1976).

The DPIC List invents a "crisis". It is tragic whenever an innocent person is convicted and sentenced to death. Obviously, it is a very serious charge to claim that 119 innocent defendants have suffered such an unjust fate. While recent developments such as DNA have revealed "wrongful convictions," the evidence does not support other claims of such miscarriages under our current capital punishment system.

In compiling its List, the DPIC has too often relied on inexact standards such as acquittals on retrial, dismissals by the prosecution, and reversals for legal insufficiency of evidence to exonerate released death row inmates. However, there is a big difference between "reasonable doubt" and the kind of "wrong person mistake" that was the genesis of the original *Stanford* study. Moreover, the DPIC has used old cases in which the defendants did not receive the modern protections that "probably reduce the likelihood of executing the innocent." It ignores the fact that the criminal justice system includes a system of review which gives defendants repeated opportunities to put the prosecution to its burden of proof.

The system has always anticipated potential factual error and has provided remedies for wrongly convicted defendants–that is why there is a more elaborate post-*Furman* trial process, an appellate process, state and federal habeas corpus processes, and clemency. The development in DNA technology is now giving birth to new post-conviction procedures in many of the states designed to give inmates the opportunity to have DNA testing that was not available at the time of their trials. Moreover, our open society promotes ongoing inquiry and investigation into legitimate claims of injustice.

However, it is irresponsible to misrepresent the extent and dimensions of this phenomenon. "It is important to preserve the distinction between acquittal and innocence, which is regularly obfuscated in news media headlines. When acquittal is interpreted as a finding of innocence, the public is led to believe that a guiltless person has been prosecuted for political or corrupt reasons." Schwartz, at 154-155. The DPIC's gimmicky and superficial List falsely inflates the problem of wrongful convictions in order to skew the public's opinion about capital punishment.

For instance, the *Cooley* article concocts the overly-dramatic, but meaningless, statistic that "one death row inmate is released because of innocence for every five inmates executed." *Cooley*, at 916. Of course, comparing an "execution" rate with a "sentenced to death" rate is mixing apples and oranges since there is no claim that any innocent defendants have actually been executed–being sentenced to death is not the same as then being executed. Yet, the recent book by Barry Scheck and Peter Neufeld, *Actual Innocence* (2000), updated this hysterical ratio to assert that one innocent inmate is being released for every seven inmates executed. This contrived "statistic" has even made its way to the Senate floor. 148 *Congressional Record* S889-92 (2/15/02). Most recently, the DPIC perpetuated this misleading comparison in its publication, *Innocence and the Crisis in the American Death Penalty* (2005) ("one exoneration for every 8 people executed").[29] The "wide use" of this dubious "new measure for evaluating the accuracy of the death penalty...." is cited as one of the events most responsible for "igniting the current capital punishment debate." 33 *Columbia Human Rights Law Rev.* 527 (2002); 63 *Ohio St. Law Journal* 343 (2002).

Of course, the valid comparison is between the total number of death sentences and the number of innocent Death Row inmates actually released from Death Row. The most recent available statistics reveal that 7,403 death sentences were imposed between 1973 and 2003.[30] Thus, even under the DPIC's own questionable estimate that 119 innocent defendants have been sentenced to death--only 1.6% of the inmates sentenced to death were released because of innocence. Of course, given the analysis in this paper, the DPIC's estimate of 119 innocent inmates is artificially inflated insofar as it may be used to evaluate our capital criminal justice system. If the 89 cases analyzed in this paper are removed from the DPIC List, then the most that can be said is that between 1973 and 2003, there were 30 wrongly convicted defendants in any meaningful sense. The possibility that less than 1/2 of 1% of the inmates sentenced to death were actually innocent does not indicate a crisis, especially when compared to the number of pre-1973 cases cited in the *Stanford* study and *In Spite of Innocence*..

The significance of these figures may be appreciated when contrasted with the DPIC's aforementioned hyperbolic ratio also used by the authors of the *Cooley* study and echoed in *Actual Innocence* and in the halls of Congress which fallaciously compares executions and exonerations. That 5:1 or 7:1 or 8:1 ratio is a nonsensical public relations statistic that creates the misimpression of an epidemic of wrongful convictions. The facts actually show that for every 7,403 death sentences imposed, 119 innocent defendants were sentenced to death or more likely it is that for the 7,403 death sentences imposed since 1973 only 40 or 31 or 11 innocent defendants have been sentenced to death. In other words, the relative number of innocent defendants sentenced to death appears to be infinitesimal.

The public may or may not take comfort from these figures. The microscopic percentage of defendants who may have been wrongly convicted and sentenced to death can be considered a testament to the accuracy and reliability of our modern capital punishment system in filtering out and punishing the actual perpetrators of our most heinous crimes. The United States Supreme Court continues to monitor and modify this system.[31]

Nevertheless, if a person believes that the death penalty should be abolished if there is any risk at all that an innocent person could be sentenced to death, then that person is justified in advocating the abolition of capital punishment. No criminal justice system can promise foolproof perfection–although the minute number of cases in which an innocent person may have been sentenced to death in this country approaches that absolute standard.

However, the inherent risk of sentencing an innocent person to death and the still unrealized possibility that an innocent person may actually be executed cannot be considered in isolation. Counterbalancing the concern that even one innocent person may be executed is the question of whether the death penalty saves innocent lives by deterring potential murderers.[32] Now, for the first time, various academic and statistical reports have been published that examine the effect of capital punishment during this modern post-*Furman* period of death penalty jurisprudence. A recent study by the Emory University Department of Economics concludes that capital punishment as it is currently administered has a strong deterrent effect, saving 8-28 lives per execution.[33] Another study conducted by School of Business & Public Adminstration at the University of Houston-Clear Lake and published in *Applied Economics* shows that homicides increase during periods when there are no executions and decrease during periods when executions are occurring. Economists with the University of Colorado at Denver studied the impact of capital punishment during the years 1977 through 1997. The preliminary results of the Colorado study indicate a deterrence effect of 5-6 fewer homicides per execution. Finally, statistical evidence has been cited to argue that the homicide rates have fallen more steadily and steeply in states that have conducted executions as opposed to states that do not conduct executions or do not have capital punishment. *The Weekly Standard*, 8/13/01. Inevitably (and properly), the debate over deterrence and the validity of these new studies will continue.[34]

Deterrence, of course, involves more than numbers. As Senator Dianne Feinstein (D.-Cal.) explained to the Senate Judiciary Committee in 1993:

"In the 1960's, I was appointed to one of the term-setting and paroling authorities and sat on some 5,000 cases of women who were convicted of felonies in the State of California. I remember one woman who came before me because she was convicted of robbery in the first degree, and I noticed on what is called the granny sheet that she had a weapon, but it was unloaded. I asked her the question why was the gun unloaded and she said, so I wouldn't panic, kill somebody and get the death penalty.

"That case went by and I didn't think too much of it at the time. I read a lot of books that said the death penalty was not a deterrent. Then in the 1970's, I walked into a mom-and-pop grocery store just after the proprietor, his wife and dog had been shot. People in real life don't die the way they do on television. There was brain matter on the ceiling, on the canned goods. It was a terrible, terrible scene of carnage.

" I came to remember that woman because by then California had done away with the death penalty. I came to remember the woman who said to me in the 1960's, the gun was unloaded so I wouldn't panic and kill someone, and suddenly the death penalty came to have new meaning to me as a deterrent."

Statement of the Honorable Dianne Feinstein, Senator from California, Hearing Before the Senate Judiciary Committee on S.221 (April 1, 1993).

As the Supreme Court conceded :"We may nevertheless assume safely that there are murderers, such as those who act in passion, for whom the threat of death has little or no deterrent effect. But for many others, the death penalty undoubtedly is a significant deterrent. There are carefully contemplated murders, such as murder for hire, where the possible penalty of death may well enter into the cold calculus that precedes the decision to act. And there are some categories of murder, such as murder by a life prisoner, where other sanctions may not be adequate." *Gregg,* 328 U.S. at 185-186 [footnotes omitted]. [35]

Under any analysis, innocent lives are at stake. On the one hand, there is the remote prospect that an innocent person may be executed despite the most elaborate, protracted, and sympathetic legal review procedures in the world. On the other, there is the possibility of innocent people horribly and brutally murdered in the streets and in their homes with no legal review process at all. When weighing these choices, the public deserves information that places the innocence question in proper perspective. The DPIC List of allegedly innocent defendants released from Death Row fails to provide that legitimate perspective.[36]

POSTSCRIPT: ACTUALLY GUILTY

Recent international interest has focused on the case of James Hanratty, one of the last murderers to be executed in England. Hanratty was hung in 1962 for the notorious "A-6 Murder". He was convicted of murdering Michael Gregsten and also raping/shooting Gregsten's girlfriend, Valerie Storie. Despite some alleged confusion about Storie's identification of him as the perpetrator, Hanratty was convicted after the longest murder trial in English history. After Hanratty was hung, another man confessed to the murder, but then recanted the confession. Hanratty's case became a *cause celebre* and was part of the final impetus leading to the abolition of the death penalty in England in 1969. Bailey, *Hangmen of England* (1992 Barnes & Noble ed.) at 190-191. The late Beatle John Lennon mourned Hanratty as a victim of "class war". However, the continuing efforts of Hanratty's supporters to "clear" his name have now come to naught. DNA evidence from Ms. Storie's underpants established Hanratty's guilt and eliminated the other alleged perpetrator who had "confessed" after Hanratty's execution. In dismissing the Hanratty family's case, the English court graciously "commend[ed] the Hanratty family for the manner in which they have logically but mistakenly pursued their long campaign to establish James Hanratty's innocence." *Regina v. James Hanratty Deceased by his Brother Michael Hanratty*, 2002 WL 499035 (May 10, 2002). Since the abolition of the death penalty, the rate of unlawful killings in Britain has soared. McKinstry, All my Life I have Been Passionately Opposed the Death Penalty . . . This is Why I have Changed My Mind, *Daily Mail*, 3/13/02. "All of us who regret the transformation of our country from a `relative oasis in violent world' to a society where crimes like the A6 murder are almost daily occurrences, are surely entitled to an apology." Hanratty Deserved to Die, *The*

Spectator (May 11, 2002) at 24-25; A recent opinion shows 81% support for restoration of capital punishment in England. *Times of London* (8/21/02).

APPENDIX-CASES RECENTLY REMOVED FROM DPIC LIST

Henry Drake--*Drake v. State,* 247 S.E.2d 57 (Ga. 1978); *Drake v. State*, 287 S.E.2d 180 (Ga. 1982); *Drake v. Francis*, 727 F.2d 990 (11th Cir. 1984); *Drake v. Kemp*, 762 F.2d 1449 (11th Cir. en banc 1985); *Campbell v. State*, 240 S.E.2d 828 (Ga. 1977). This case is yet another example of release due to witness recantation, not actual innocence. Drake and William Campbell were tried separately for the murder of a local barber.

The elderly barber was violently assaulted in his shop with a knife and a claw hammer. There were pools of blood and blood smears on the wall of his barber shop. There were two pocket knives on top of the blood on the floor. One of the knives was similar to one owned by Drake.

When first arrested, Campbell implicated Drake as the murderer and stated he (Campbell) was not present. Campbell then told his own attorney that he (Campbell) alone was guilty of the murder and that Drake was innocent. Campbell actually offered many different versions to his lawyer before settling on a story that did not implicate Drake. However, Campbell then took the stand at his own trial (which occurred before Drake's) and testified, to his attorney's surprise, that Drake attacked the barber while Campbell was getting a haircut. Campbell was nonetheless convicted of the barber's murder and sentenced to death.

Subsequently, Campbell reluctantly testified at Drake's trial and implicated Drake. The prosecution's theory was that Campbell, an older man in ill-health with emphysema, could not have murdered the barber by himself. After Drake was convicted and sentenced to death, Campbell recanted his testimony against Drake. However, his newest version of events also differed from Drake's own testimony. Furthermore, the testimony of Drake's girlfriend had also differed from Drake's testimony. The trial court rejected Campbell's recantation and Campbell died soon thereafter.

Drake's first conviction was reversed and in two subsequent retrials, two different juries heard Campbell's recantation and also heard forensic evidence that was offered to contradict the prosecution's theory that the barber was attacked by two assailants. One jury hung in favor of acquittal, but a second jury convicted Drake again. Five former jurors from Drake's original trial also advised the parole board that Campbell's recantation would not have changed their verdict convicting Drake at his first trial. Nevertheless, in a decision uncritically accepted by the DPIC, the state parole board "simply decided Drake was innocent." *Atlanta Journal-Constitution*, 12/24/87; *Los Angeles Times,* 12/22/88, 12/23/88. Notwithstanding the parole board's decision,

Campbell's numerous statements and recantations, which did not even always agree with Drake's version of events, do not establish Drake's actual innocence.

In addition, Drake was no longer on Death Row at the time the parole board acted in his case. He was serving a life sentence. The Eleventh Circuit Court of Appeals vacated his original conviction and sentence on grounds of prosecutorial misconduct and instructional error. When Drake was retried, he received only a life sentence.

John Henry Knapp--Knapp had three trials for the house fire murder of his daughters. Knapp stood outside and cooly watched his daughters be incinerated while sipping hot coffee. In the first trial, the jury hung 7-5 for conviction. The second trial resulted in a conviction and death sentence, but was reversed because of newly-developed evidence that indicated that the fatal fire could have been accidentally set by his dead daughters. Nonetheless, the third trial still ended in a mistrial with the jury hung 7-5 for conviction. The evidence included Knapp's recanted confession which he claimed he made because he suffered a migraine headache and was trying to protect his wife.

Finally, the prosecution concluded that the evidence was insufficient to obtain a unanimous jury verdict of guilt or innocence. The case was 19 years old and there had been losses in "some key evidence and witnesses." Knapp then pled "no contest" to second degree murder and received a sentence of time served. The judge who presided at Knapp's first two trials indicated doubts about Knapp's guilt, but still said that the fire was purposely set by **either** Knapp or his wife. "Given the original evidence and subsequent proceedings in the case, we may never know if Knapp was guilty . . . ". 33 *Ariz.T.L.J.* 665, 666 (2001). Under the DPIC's current standards, Knapp's name should not be on the DPIC List since he pled to a lesser offense. *Arizona Republic* (8/27/91,11/19/92, 11/20/92,8/11/96); *Phoenix Gazette (*12/6/91, 11/20/92); *Associated Press* (11/19/92). \

Jerry Bigelow-- *Bigelow v. Superior Court (People)*, 204 Cal.App.3d 1127 (1988). Bigelow's conviction and death sentence were reversed for a reasons unrelated to his guilt. On retrial, the jury convicted Bigelow of robbery and kidnaping. The jury also found true that the murder occurred while Bigelow was committing or was an accomplice in the robbery and kidnaping of the victim. In short, the jury found true beyond a reasonable doubt all the facts necessary to convict Bigelow of first degree felony murder under California law. Nonetheless, the jury did not actually convict Bigelow of the separate charge of first degree murder. The trial judge made the mistake of excusing the jury without clarifying its inconsistent verdict. Therefore, under California law, the verdicts had to be entered and Bigelow was not eligible for the death penalty. However, rather than establishing that Bigelow was innocent, the jury's verdicts still indicated that the jury totally rejected Bigelow's defense and found that he was at least an accomplice to the murder. An inconsistent verdict, such as Bigelow's, is not an exoneration. "Inconsistent verdicts" are often a product of jury leniency, rather than a belief in innocence. Nonetheless, the prosecution cannot appeal an inconsistent verdict. *United*

States v. Powell, 469 U.S. 57, 65-66 (1984). As noted, the jury's verdict also indicates that, at a minimum, it believed that Bigelow was an accomplice to the murder. Originally, this factual distinction between actual perpetrator and accomplice was not considered proof of "actual innocence". *Stanford*, at 43.

William Jent &

Earnest Miller --These co-defendants entered pleas to lesser offenses of second degree murder and were sentenced to time served after their convictions were vacated because of the prosecution's failure to disclose exculpatory evidence. Although Jent and Miller proclaimed their innocence, they inconsistently asked for the "pardon" of the victim's family. It appears that the passage of time made a second trial problematic for both the prosecution **and** the defense. The prosecution had lost its key physical evidence and witnesses were scattered. Several witnesses had changed their testimony. *Associated Press*, 1/15/88, 1/16/88; *St. Petersburg Times*, 1/16/88, 1/19/88. Under the DPIC's current standards, these cases should not be on the DPIC List since the two men pled to lesser charges. In a statement to the Florida Commission on Capital Cases, the prosecution cited conflicting statements from Miller and Jent about their alibi to contradict assertions that the defendants did have an alibi for this murder.

Jesse Keith Brown–*State v. Brown*, 347 S.E.2d 882 (S.C. 1986); *State v. Brown*, 371 S.E.2d 523 (S.C. 1988). This defendant was acquitted at his second retrial because evidence also pointed to his half brother as the "actual killer". However, the jury also convicted Brown of armed robbery, grand larceny, and entering without breaking in connection with the homicide. The verdict indicates, therefore, that Brown was involved in the murder even if he was not actual perpetrator. Indeed, at his first trial he testified that he did not remember committing the murder, but was "sorry [if I've done anything]." At his second trial, on the other hand, he testified specifically that he was not involved in the murder. Brown's case was not included in *In Spite of Innocence*, thus this appears to be one of the unidentified cases in which the *Cooley* study considered the evidence of innocence to be "relatively weak." *Cooley*, at p. 914, 928-929. Moreover, the double reversals of Brown's first two trials indicate that it is speculative that Brown would have ever been sentenced to death at all if his initial trial had not been conducted erroneously]

Patrick Croy-- *People v. Croy*, 41 Cal.3d 1 (Cal. 1986). Croy was convicted of murdering a police officer in Yreka, California. The California Supreme Court reversed Croy's murder conviction for instructional error, but it affirmed his conviction for conspiracy to commit murder. His defense had been intoxication. Yet, on retrial, Croy claimed self-defense and was acquitted of murder. Thus, Croy was not "actually innocent" in the sense of being the wrong person.

There was no dispute Croy killed the police officer. However, he was acquitted on the basis of a controversial and legally questionable cultural defense based on his Native American heritage, i.e., that his background as a Native American led him to *reasonably fear that the police officer intended to kill him. See, e.g.,* Comment, *99 Dick.L.Rev.* 141 (1994); 13 *Ariz.J.Int'l & Comp.L.* 523 (1996); Note, 62 *Ohio St. L.J.* 1695 (2001); Note, 2001 *Duke L.J.* 1809 (2001).

By contrast (and inconsistently), at his first trial, Croy did not claim self-defense. Instead, he relied on an extensive intoxication defense and testified that he initially "became concerned when he saw the police because he was on probation and was afraid that he would be arrested for being drunk." He also claimed "he was startled when [the police officer/victim] appeared as he was trying to find safety in his grandmother's cabin, and that if he shot [the victim] he did not intend to." *People v. Croy* (1986) 41 Cal.3d 1, 16, 19, 21. The defenses Croy used at his first and second trials were inconsistent with each other.

Croy's testimony at his second trial was not all that impressive either. While he testified emotionally that he believed the police "were going to kill us all", other parts of his testimony sounded like a "prepared statement" and he was forced to admit that he had consumed an "impressive amount of liquor and marijuana" during the fateful weekend he confronted the police. Croy admitted lying at his first trial, but explained that he lied because did not believe he could win and he wanted to protect his friends. "All in all, Croy's performance was neither as commanding as [his attorney] hoped it would be, nor as damaging as the prosecution tried to make it. As the long trial drew to a close..., it seemed that victory...would depend less on [Croy's] courtroom 'vibrations', than on the [defense] attorney's to indict Yreka as a racist community."

Croy's second trial was depicted as a political trial, not a trial about guilt or innocence. "What made...Croy worthy in his attorney's mind was not so much his innocence as his symbolic value as an aggrieved Indian [sic]...." More significantly, neither defense at Croy's two trials established that Croy was "actually innocent" or the "wrong person". *Los Angeles Times* (5/11/00); *San Francisco Examiner* (7/8/90); *Santa Rosa Press Democrat*, (7/27/97).

[1] Supervising Deputy Attorney General, State of California. Member, Association of Government Attorneys in Capital Litigation (AGACL). The writer represents the State in death penalty appeals and is a supporter of the death penalty. This paper was the basis for a presentation at an annual meeting of AGACL during 2002 and for use by the California District Attorneys Association as part of a Death Penalty White Paper. An earlier

version of this paper was also appended to the Minority Report of the United States Senate Judiciary Committee concerning S. 486 ("The Innocence Protection Act') (2002). However, this work represents solely the views of its author and is not an official publication of the California Department of Justice nor does it represent the views of AGACL. This paper is updated and revised as events warrant. The author and/or this report also been cited in Cohen, *The Wrong Men* (2003), the *Federal Lawyer*, the *New York Times*, the *Chicago Tribune, National Review Online,* and *USA Today.*

[2] The DPIC recently

[3]The DPIC List is located at its website: http://www.deathpenaltyinfo.org/innoc.html

[4] Citations in this study are to the 1994 paperback edition published by Northeastern University Press.

[5] The *Stanford* study includes historically controversial defendants such as Bruno Hauptmann, executed for the kidnapping and murder of the Lindbergh baby, and Dr. Sam Sheppard, ultimately acquitted on retrial for the murder of his wife, as examples of wrongfully convicted murderers. However, the most recent study of Hauptmann's case supports the evidence of his conviction. Fisher, *The Ghosts of Hopewell* (Southern Ill. Univ. Press 1999). Similarly, the most recent civil litigation concerning the conviction of the late Dr. Sheppard rejected evidence of his innocence. *Cleveland Plain Dealer* (4/13/00).

[6] The 416 number is cited in the Introduction and apparently does not include an additional 7 cases cited in the preface to the 1994 paperback edition of the book. *In Spite of Innocence,* at xi.

[7] *Cooley* itself only lists 68 defendants. The DPIC does not explain how it has otherwise learned of the cases or defendants it has since added to its current list of 102 defendants.

[8] Since then, of course, DPIC has added three additional names for a total of 119 "Inmates Freed from Death Row."

[9] In previous drafts of this paper and presentations on this subject, this writer had argued that all six of these defendants should be deleted from the DPIC List. Descriptions of these six cases are appended to this paper.

[10] Significantly, the overwhelming number of cases cited in the widely-published *In Spite of Innocence* involve cases that occurred in the pre-*Furman* period.

[11] For example, the Court has held that defendants who were younger than 18 at the time of their offenses cannot be executed. *Roper v. Simmons*, _U.S._, 125 S.Ct. 1183 (2005). For purposes of assessing whether innocent defendants have been sentenced to death, both of these cases may indicate that certain defendants currently on the DPIC List would not have been or should not have been eligible for the death penalty at all.

[12] For instance, the original DPIC Report, *Innocence and the Death Penalty: Assessing the Danger of Mistaken Executions* (1993), went to great length to explain the obstacles facing defendants in proving their "innocence" (i.e. the defendant did not commit the crime) after conviction.

[13] The DPIC has now removed prisoners who received lesser charges.

[14] As will be shown, some states have exceptions to this general rule of appellate review which favor the defendant.

[15] An example of such a difference relates to convictions based on accomplice testimony. A conviction based solely on accomplice testimony is insufficient for a conviction in California unless it is corroborated by some other evidence. However, a conviction on accomplice testimony would be sufficient in federal court even without corroboration. *Laboa v. Calderon*, 224 F.3d 972 (9th Cir. 2000).

[16] Furthermore, when a defendant secures a new trial on grounds of ineffective assistance of counsel or because the prosecution has improperly withheld material, exculpatory evidence, he is not required to prove that he is innocent or even that he would have been acquitted. In fact, he does not need to even prove that it is "more likely than not" that he would be acquitted--found not guilty under a "reasonable doubt" standard. He need only show a "reasonable probability" that the outcome would have been different--he need only undermine confidence in the guilt verdict in his case. *Strickland v. Washington*, 466 U.S. 668, 693-694 (1984); *United States v. Bagley*. 473 U.S. 667, 679-682 (1985). If a prosecutor presents perjured testimony, the conviction is reversed if there is any reasonable likelihood the verdict would be different. *Bagley*, at 679-680. Although a defendant may get a new trial because of these claims, none of these standards amount to a finding of the defendant's "actual innocence". For that matter, if a defendant secures a new trial because his counsel failed to move to suppress incriminating evidence or because the defendant confessed to a jailhouse inmate who was working as a police agent, he may be acquitted or charges may be dismissed because the prosecution has been prevented from introducing relevant, reliable evidence of guilt. *Kimmelman v. Morrison,* 477 U.S. 365, 391-398 (Powell, J. conc.) (the defendant benefits from the "windfall" that evidence of guilt is suppressed); *In re Neely*, 6 Cal.4th 901, 922-925 (Arabian, J. conc.) (suppression of tape recording of defendant's admissions renders retrial "inherently less reliable").

[17] No matter how the DPIC defines its criteria, its List and similar analyses are continually misinterpreted as meaning that the "wrong person" was convicted in every case. For instance, Senator Leahy has used the DPIC List to assert the following: "When dozens of innocent people are being sentenced to death, and dozens of guilty people are working [walking] free because the State has convicted the wrong person, we must ask ourselves what went wrong in that trial process...." 146 Cong. Rec. S4669-03, S4675 (6/7/00). Similarly, "[t]here is one other thing we should keep in mind. If the wrong person is on death row for a murder, if somebody is convicted of a murder they did not commit, that means that the real murderer is still running loose. Maybe everybody can feel comfortable that we have locked up somebody for the murder, but if there is still a killer on the loose, everything has broken down. Not only is an innocent man on death row, but a guilt man is running free." 148 Cong. Rec. S889-02, S891 (2/15/02). As explained in the text, the fact that a defendant is acquitted or a case is dismissed does not necessarily mean that a "guilty person" is still "walking free" or "running loose". As recently as 2004, information from the DPIC List and similar studies was still relied upon fallaciously to assert: "What's more, the conviction of these innocent people inflicted needless harm on the criminal justice system because every time an innocent person is convicted, that means the guilty person who committed the rape or the murder or the robbery has not been caught and is out committing other crimes." (Prof. Samuel Gross, Univ. of Mich. Law School, NPR, 4/20/04, 2004 WL 56756464).

[18] The DPIC has now removed such defendants from its List.

[19] Of course, it is problematic to draw conclusions about a defendant's guilt and innocence by comparing the results in that defendant's trials and retrials. Many variables, rather than a single piece of evidence or one particular witness, may explain differences in outcomes. See also *People v. Marshall,* 13 Cal.4th 799, 842 fn. 7 (1996); *People v. Burch* (1961) 196 Cal.App.2d 754, 772 (1961); see also *United States v. Zuno-Arce*, 44 F.3d 1420, 1423 (9th Cir. 1995).

[20] This is not to say that the incidence of "trial error" in capital cases is irrelevant to the capital punishment debate. Totally separate studies, which have also generated controversy about their methodology, have been directed at that issue. For the time being, however, the problem of reversible errors in death penalty litigation is outside the scope of this paper.

[21] This is not to say that there are not instances when "actual innocence" is proved as part of the reviewing process itself. There are occasions when "newly discovered" or "newly developed" evidence, such as DNA, is introduced as part of the post-conviction process demonstrates that the "wrong person" is on Death Row. Inmates "exonerated" in this fashion are properly included on the DPIC List.

[22] These "better result after reversal" cases should be distinguished from those in which the government suppressed exculpatory or mitigating evidence or defense counsel's incompetence precluded uncovering exonerating evidence until long after the trial or the end of the review process. They should also to be distinguished from those cases in which genuine newly-discovered or newly-developed evidence of innocence is found after the trial, such as the recent advances in DNA technology. These events, which have happened only rarely despite the DPIC List's claims to the contrary, will usually constitute authentic cases of "actual innocence" involving defendants mistakenly and unjustly placed on Death Row. Finally, the reversed/acquitted on retrial cases should be distinguished from cases in which the prosecution does choose not to retry cases because the prosecution has concluded that the defendant is innocent.

[23] The writer has also been aided by information recently compiled by the Florida Commission on Capital Crimes, the Journal of the DuPage County Bar Association, and the Philadelphia District Attorney's office. I am also grateful for the advice and counsel of colleagues and friends interested in this subject.

[24] Even the sympathetic district court which held the federal death penalty invalid because of the danger of "wrongful convictions" agreed that the DPIC methodology was overinclusive. *United States v. Quinones,* 205 F.Supp.2d 256, 265 (S.D.N.Y. 2002) [hereinafter *Quinones I]* reversed *United States v. Quinones,*313 F.3d 49 (2nd Cir. 2002) [hereinafter *Quinones II*] cert. den. *Quinones v. United States,* 540 U.S. 1051 (2003). After examining at least 101 descriptions on the DPIC List, the court exercised undefined "conservative criterion" to agree that only 31of the named defendants were "factually innocent." The court also speculated that 8 other defendants had substantial arguments. *Quinones I,* at 265 & fn. 11. Without explanation, the district court also expressed satisfaction that the DPIC used "reasonably strict and objective standards in listing and describing the data and summaries that appear on its website." Ibid. The court did not explain its conclusion. Indeed, in an earlier opinion, the same court had noted that the "basis of the exoneration" for some of the cases on the DPIC List "is not clearly discernible." *United States v. Quinones,* 196 F.Supp.2d 416, 418 fn. 5 (S.D.N.Y. 2002)

[25] This study is not exhaustive, but is based on materials available to the author. These materials are cited in the summaries and also include the *Stanford* study, *In Spite of Innocence,* the *Cooley* article, and the summaries available on the DPIC website. It is not conceded that other defendants on the DPIC List who are not mentioned in this study are actually innocent. For that matter, the writer is always interested in additional information bearing on any defendant's claim of "actual innocence".

[26] Governor Ryan pardoned Rolando Cruz in 2002. The prosecution argued that unanswered questions remained about Cruz's actual involvement in the Nicarico murder. *Chicago Tribune* (11/15/02); *Associated Press* (11/15/02). Illinois prosecutors are reportedly preparing a case agains Dugan. *Arlington Heights Daily Herald* (2/26/05).

[27] Gov. Ryan of Illinois pardoned Gauger in 2002. The prosecution opposed the pardon request on grounds that there were still unanswered questions about Gauger's possible involvement in his parents' murder. *Associated Press* (11/15/02).

[28] The appeals court holding about the tape was not binding on the trial court. Thus, the trial court judge had the discretion on retrial to exclude the entire tape. The prosecution would not have been able to appeal the trial court's ruling. The Martinez acquittal could have boiled down to no more than a disagreement between the prosecution and the trial court about the audibility of a tape.

[29]Interestingly, even on its own terms, this latest computation actually represents an improvement in the ratio of innocent to executed..

[30] The total number of death sentences since 2003 is not yet available. Of course, the number of death sentences dwarfs the total number of post-1972 executions (972). By choosing this much smaller number of actual executions, the DPIC inflates the statistical significance of its list. The DPIC also falsely enhances the ratio by including cases involving defendants who could not have been executed under the post-1972 death penalty laws. The DPIC offers no rationale for including these old cases in its List.

[31] For instance, the High Court declared it unconstitutional to execute the mentally retarded or murderers who committed their crimes when under the age of 18.

[32] By focusing on the deterrence aspects of capital punishment, this writer is not ignoring that for many people there are reasons for supporting and opposing the death penalty that are totally irrelevant to the deterrence issue.

[33] The Emory study itself notes potential problems with some of these other studies. However, the objectivity of some these studies is underscored by the ambivalence expressed about the death penalty by several of the academicians who compiled the information. For instance, the Emory study warns: "[D]eterrence reflects social benefits associated with the death penalty, but one should also weigh in the corresponding social costs. These include the regret associated with the irreversible decision to execute an innocent person. Moreover, issues such as the possible unfairness of the justice system and discrimination need to be considered when making a social decision regarding capital punishment." The Colorado working paper concludes with a similar caveat about other "significant issues" including racial discrimination in the imposition of the death penalty and the pardon process. "Given these concerns, a stand for or against capital punishment should be taken with caution." Thus, the researchers who have prepared these most recent deterrence studies do not appear predisposed to supporting the death penalty.

[34] An exhaustive listing of these recent studies may be found at the Criminal Justice Legal Foundation website (http://www.cjlf.org/deathpenalty/DPDeterrence.htm). They are also cited in Marquis, *The Myth of Innocence*, 95 J. Crim.L & Criminology 501, 505 fn.29 (Winter 2005). These studies are also discussed in Sunstein-Vermeule, *Is Capital Punishment Morally Required? The Relevance of Life-Life Tradeoffs*, Working Paper 05-06, AEI Brookings Joint Center for Regulatory Studies (March 2005). The debate is being joined already. See the DPIC website about deterrence.

[35] Moreover, case law is replete with examples of the ineffectiveness of imprisonment as a deterrent to murder. See, e.g. *Tison v.* Arizona, 481 U.S. 137 (1987) (recounting the bloody family assisted escape of a life termer already serving time for an escape/murder); *Campbell v. Kincheloe*, 829 F.2d 1453 (9th Cir. 1987)(prison escapee commits triple murder of witnesses who testified against him); *Hernandez v. Johnson*, 108 F.3d 554 (5th Cir. 1997) (twice-convicted murderer murders jail guard during abortive jail escape); *People v. Allen*, 42 Cal.3d 1222 (Cal. 1986) (murderer serving life sentence convicted of murdering witness on the outside, murder of two bystanders, and conspiracy to murder seven other prior witnesses) aff'd *Allen v. Woodford* 395 F.3d 979, 1019 (9th Cir. 2005) ("Given the nature of his crimes, sentencing him to another life term would achieve none of the traditional purposes underlying punishment.Allen continues to pose a threat to society, indeed to those very persons who testified against him in the Fran's Market triple-murder trial here at issue, and has proven that he is beyond rehabilitation. He has shown himself more than capable of arranging murders from behind bars. If the death penalty is to serve any purpose at all, it is to prevent the very sort of murderous conduct for which Allen was convicted.)

[36] "[I]f findings [about deterrence] are ultimately shown to be right, capital punishment has a strong claim to being, not merely morally permissible, but morally obligatory, above all from the standpoint of those who wish to protect life." Sunstein, at p. 42.

Mr. COBLE. Thank you very much, Mr. Marquis. And for my geographic edification, Mr. Marquis, from where does your wife hail in North Carolina?

Mr. MARQUIS. Charlotte, sir.

Mr. COBLE. That is our largest city.

Mr. MARQUIS. And my parents went to school at Black Mountain.

Mr. COBLE. I know it well.

Mr. Eisenberg.

TESTIMONY OF RON EISENBERG, DEPUTY DISTRICT ATTORNEY, PHILADELPHIA, PENNSYLVANIA

Mr. EISENBERG. Thank you, Mr. Chairman, and Members of the Committee. Mr. Chairman, for your information, my wife actually lives in Greensboro at this moment, and I hope to be able to join her there in the future.

Mr. COBLE. My district, and I will give you all the time you want.

Mr. EISENBERG. Mr. Chairman, I have served as a prosecutor for 24 years. I am the supervisor in the law division in the Philadelphia District Attorney's Office. It is a group of 60 lawyers. Many of them handle regular State court appeals, but more and more of them have to devote themselves exclusively to Federal habeas corpus work. In fact, in the last decade the number of lawyers handling just Federal habeas corpus review of State court convictions in my office has increased by 400 percent.

Now, too often the debate about the proper scope of Federal habeas corpus review comes down to disagreement about the value of the death penalty and the justice of imprisonment and punishment generally. And to be sure, many Federal courts seem flatly unwilling to affirm capital sentences. That is certainly true of my jurisdiction in Pennsylvania where almost every single contested death sentence litigated on habeas corpus review has been overturned by Federal courts; over 20 cases, only one has been affirmed. But the problem I want to address today is not simply one of results, and Federal court intrusion to State court convictions cannot be justified either by opposition to the death penalty or as vindication of civil rights. The truth is that whether or not they actually reverse a conviction, Federal habeas corpus courts drag out litigation for years of unjustifiable delay, creating exorbitant cost for the State and endless pain for the victims.

We have detailed several of these cases in my written testimony, Your Honor. The most prominent and perhaps our most prominent death penalty defender from Philadelphia is a cop killer named Mumia Abu-Jamal. Now he has become a famous person around the world. There is a lot of disagreement about his alleged innocence, but we are just trying to get his case litigated through the courts.

This murder occurred in 1981. It was just around the time when I started in the DA's office. I helped work on the trial of that case, and now I am working on his Federal habeas corpus review, and we're not close to done. Several years ago a United States District Court judge granted him a new sentencing hearing, threw out the death penalty but affirmed the conviction, rejecting all of his claims of innocence. That was in 2001—that ruling was in 2001. We appealed it, and we haven't even gotten close to a ruling yet. In fact, the court hasn't even allowed us to file our briefs in that case almost 4 years later. That is on top of the two decades of delay we had before we even got to that ruling in 2001 in this case. Now it is closing in on 25 years, haven't been able to file our briefs in the Third Circuit Court of Appeals.

We have several other cases of the same nature where cases sit for years waiting for elementary procedural steps to occur in Federal court, not just for decisions to be made, not just for briefs to be mulled over and carefully considered, but even for elementary preliminary decisions to be made about allowing the filing of papers. This happens in case after case, and it happens even in cases, as we have detailed in the written testimony, where the defendant himself doesn't want to challenge his conviction. Where even the defendant says, I want to give up my Federal habeas corpus appeals, the Federal courts will not allow him to, and lengthen and stretch out the litigation, despite the wishes of the defendant himself.

Now, from talking to my colleagues around the country, I know that their experiences are similar, and I think that these cases demonstrate the inherent imbalance in the exercise of Federal habeas corpus review over State criminal convictions.

Federal courts have great power simply because they're last in line when it comes to our cases, but they have little responsibility because they're so far removed in time and space from the circumstances of the crime and the subtleties of the State proceedings. Accordingly, they have small motive to act expeditiously or efficiently to give credit to the judgments of their brethren in the State courts or to consider the needs of crime victims.

Bill No. 3035, the "Streamlined Procedures Act of 2005," will address all of those issues and will prevent Federal courts from stretching out these cases in ways that no one on either side of the underlying questions can really debate, it seems to me. Whether you are against the death penalty or for it, I don't know how you justify a case like Mumia Abu-Jamal sitting waiting for a briefing to occur for 4 years. That is the kind of reform that this bill will enact, and we urge your support.

Thank you.

[The prepared statement of Mr. Eisenberg follows:]

PREPARED STATEMENT OF RONALD EISENBERG

I am a deputy district attorney in Pennsylvania, and I am here to talk about what really happens when state court convictions are subjected to habeas corpus review in the federal courts.

I have served as a prosecutor for 24 years. I am the supervisor of the Law Division of the Philadelphia District Attorney's Office, a group of 60 lawyers. Many of those lawyers handle regular appeals in the Pennsylvania appellate courts. But more and more of our attorneys must devote themselves full time to federal habeas corpus litigation. In the last decade, the number of lawyers employed exclusively on habeas work has increased 400%. The convictions that reach federal habeas review are for the most serious crimes that can be committed against a human being—murder, rape, violent robberies and burglaries, serious beatings and shootings.

Too often, the debate about the proper scope of federal habeas corpus review comes down to disagreement about the value of the death penalty, and the justness of imprisonment and punishment generally. To be sure, many federal courts seem flatly unwilling to affirm capital sentences. In Pennsylvania, for example, almost every single contested death sentence litigated on habeas—over 20 cases in the last decade—has been thrown out by federal judges; only one has been upheld.

But the problem is not simply one of results, and federal court intrusion into state convictions cannot be justified either by opposition to the death penalty or as vindication of civil rights. The truth is that, whether or not they actually reverse a conviction, federal habeas courts drag out litigation for years of utterly unjustifiable delay, creating exorbitant costs for the state and endless pain for the victims. Here are just a few examples of what it's like.

Mumia Abu-Jamal

Over two decades ago, in December 1981, Mumia Abu-Jamal murdered Officer Danny Faulkner during a traffic stop. First he shot the officer in the back; then, after the officer fell to the ground, he shot him in the face. In 2001, after twenty years of litigation, a federal district judge upheld the first degree murder conviction but overturned the sentence of death. Both sides appealed. And there the matter has sat for going on four years. No decision; no oral argument; not even a briefing schedule, which is normally the very first step in the appellate process.

The defendant has become famous over all this time; he has managed to turn himself into a celebrity. But no matter where one comes down on this case, how is it possible to justify a federal habeas process that does not even begin to resolve an appeal—let alone actually resolve it—after four years' time? Even if one buys Mumia's ever-changing, bogus claims of innocence, why does he sit in jail while nothing happens? And what about the widow Danny Faulkner left behind?

William Holland

This kind of delay is hardly unique to high-profile cases like Jamal. William Holland is not famous. Holland broke into the home of a woman in 1984. He tied her up, raped her, and stabbed her repeatedly. The victim was 71 years old. Holland had two full rounds of appeals in state court, but his claims were unsuccessful. A federal court judge nonetheless threw out his death sentence in 2001. The prosecution immediately appealed. And ever since, the federal appeals court has been dallying about what issues it will allow the defendant to raise—if and when it ever gets around to looking at any. No briefs have been filed, no argument has been held, no decision has been rendered.

Joseph Kindler

In 1982, Joseph Kindler kidnapped a witness who was scheduled to testify against him in a burglary trial. Kindler beat the man over the head with a baseball bat, hit him with an electric prod, put him in the trunk of a car, drove him to a river, tied a cinder block around his neck, and drowned him. After his conviction and sentence of death, Kindler sawed through a barred window and escaped from prison. He fled to Canada, which has no death penalty. After his arrest there, he escaped from prison again, and was re-apprehended only after his appearance on "America's Most Wanted." He then fought extradition for several years, until his eventual (and quite involuntary) return to this country.

Once back, Kindler pursued appeals, but the state courts ruled that he had forfeited his right to do so by virtue of his escapes from legal process. The federal habeas courts, to which Kindler turned in 1999, were more indulgent. The district court immediately granted a stay of execution, even though the state had not yet scheduled any execution. The prosecution appealed the stay, the parties filed briefs—and nothing happened. Two years later, after prodding by the prosecution, the federal appeals court finally scheduled oral argument in 2001, vacated the stay of execution, and sent the case back to the lower court to consider the legal claims that had been rejected by the state courts.

True to form, the lower federal court then overturned Kindler's death sentence, after two more years of litigation. The state appealed this 2003 ruling, and the case has now been pending on appeal for another two years.

Donald Hardcastle

During a burglary in 1982, Donald Hardcastle murdered an elderly couple and set their house on fire. Each victim had been stabbed over 30 times. Hardcastle unsuccessfully appealed in state court, two separate times. He started a federal habeas action in 1998, and three years later the federal judge threw out the conviction entirely. We challenged that ruling and received a partial victory—after another three years of litigation—when the federal appeals court told the district judge to start over, ruling that he should at least have granted us a hearing before automatically accepting all the defendant's factual allegations as true.

By then it was the year 2004. After yet another adverse ruling by the district judge, we appealed again. The appeals court has not yet allowed briefing, and there has been no action whatever on this case for the past six months—a period of time longer than many appeals take from start to finish.

Brian Thomas

Brian Thomas sexually assaulted and murdered a woman in 1985, with a crutch. The crutch was used to penetrate the victim's body through the vagina and rectum, while she was still alive, causing a massive tear that extended into the chest cavity. Thomas was convicted and sentenced to death, and the sentence was upheld through two separate rounds of appeal in state court.

Thomas filed a federal habeas petition in 2000. There was then briefing, counter-briefing, and counter-counter-briefing before the federal district judge, which took three years. At that point the federal judge took no action on the matter at all for another year and a half. Just this month the habeas judge finally issued an order. But the order neither grants nor denies the habeas petition. Instead the judge has merely scheduled the case for oral argument—18 months after the last briefs were filed with him.

Michael Pierce

Federal habeas litigation ensures undue delay not only at the expense of victims and prosecutors, but even, in many cases, against the wishes of the defendants themselves. Michael Pierce is one such case. Pierce repeatedly argued with his parents and threatened to kill them. After they kicked him out of their house, he set it on fire with a can of gasoline while they were inside. His mother and father died, along with his 95-year-old grandmother. The crime occurred in 1989.

From the time of the trial, Pierce declined to make the usual claim in capital cases—mental infirmity. He chose not to allow his lawyers to secure records or experts for the purpose of creating a psychological defense. The state courts upheld his conviction and sentence, ruling that Pierce's lawyers did not act improperly by accepting rather than overriding his decision.

On federal habeas corpus review, initiated in 2002, a new set of defense lawyers attempted to circumvent Pierce's desires and the ruling of the state courts. At the lawyers' request, a federal judge issued an order directing state corrections officials to remove Pierce from prison and transport him to a hospital chosen by the lawyers, to undergo testing by experts hired by the lawyers. The judge thereafter required state officials to place Pierce in an involuntary mental health commitment.

All this was done without any previous finding that Pierce was incompetent, or any hearing concerning his mental status. Indeed the habeas court initially entered its order ex parte—without any notice to the prosecution, or even to the defendant. The court explicitly directed the state prison officials to keep the whole affair secret from prosecutors. We found out about it only after the ex parte order was inadvertently placed on the public court docket. We then appealed.

Shortly after the appeal was filed, the federal court directed the parties to address as a preliminary matter whether the timing of the appeal was procedurally proper. That was in March 2004. Since then, a period of 15 months, the appeal has remained pending; in fact the court has been completely silent, making no decision about whether it will even let the appeal proceed. If the appeal is dismissed, Pierce will be automatically subject to the district judge's orders, and the court presumably will, at some point years in the future, rule on the sentence.

Hubert Michael

Hubert Michael's is another case illustrating the intrusiveness of the federal habeas process. In 1993, Michael kidnapped a 16-year-old girl and took her to a remote rural area. There he shot her with a .44 magnum handgun: once in the chest, once in the back, and once in the back of the head. His explanation for the killing was that he felt resentment toward women generally because he had been charged in an unrelated rape case.

At trial, after an extensive colloquy, Michael chose to plead guilty to first degree murder. Later, at a separate sentencing hearing, and after consultation with counsel, he elected not to present mitigation evidence, and received the death penalty. On his automatic direct appeal, he indicated his desire that the sentence be affirmed. A collateral petition was subsequently filed in state court on his behalf. Michael sought to withdraw it, and after a hearing determined that he was fully competent, his request was granted. On appeal the state supreme court, in an abundance of caution, addressed and denied as meritless all the claims raised by counsel.

Meanwhile Michael's attorneys filed a federal habeas petition on his behalf. He sent letters to the habeas court asking to withdraw the petition and dismiss counsel. The federal court insisted on another mental health review. After three more years of litigation, the court found that Michael was indeed competent, and dismissed his habeas petition as requested.

The federal appeals court refused to accept this result. The court appointed counsel for Michael over his objection, and asked him again, after warning him of the consequences, whether he wished to withdraw his appeals. Michaels said clearly that he did. Apparently that was the "wrong" answer. The appeals court responded with a ruling that, since Michael had a lawyer, his own desires must be disregarded, and his habeas corpus petition had to proceed. For good measure the appeals court told the district judge to ignore any future similar assertions by Michael. That is where the matter stands, after 12 years of insistence by Michael that he does not wish to challenge his conviction.

Lisa Lambert

The case that perhaps best epitomizes intrusiveness and delay by federal habeas corpus courts is not even a death penalty. Lisa Lambert was a high school teenager whose former boyfriend had transferred his attentions to another girl. Lambert was furious. She began to stalk and harass the other girl. Finally, just before Christmas in 1991, Lambert entered the victim's home with two cohorts in tow and confronted her. Then she slit her throat. Lambert was convicted of first degree murder. Her appeal in state court was denied.

Lambert filed a federal habeas petition in 1996, and the federal judge promptly appointed her a high-powered law firm. Within days of the filing of an amended petition, the court ordered a conference and scheduled an evidentiary hearing—even though none of the legal claims had yet been raised in state court, as required by law. Within three months (an amazing speed record in a habeas case) the judge had overturned Lambert's murder conviction and released her onto the street. In doing so he declared her actually "innocent"—even though she admitted that she had participated in the crime, and merely quibbled about the degree of her culpability. The habeas judge also explicitly condemned the state prosecutor and police, accused them of gross misconduct, and attempted to initiate a federal criminal investigation against them.

On appeal, the federal appellate court reversed, ruling that Lambert had to go back to state court first. The state trial judge—who is now himself a federal judge—then held a months-long evidentiary hearing, and wrote a 200-page opinion. In it he meticulously examined and debunked the various assertions that had been put forth by Lambert and so easily accepted by the federal habeas judge. The state judge's conclusions were in turn upheld in an 80-page opinion of the Pennsylvania appellate court.

Lambert then came right back to federal habeas court. There the previously assigned judge announced his intention to ignore everything that had happened in state court, and to release the "innocent" defendant all over again. In the end, however, the judge was compelled to disqualify himself. Another judge was assigned. This judge upheld the conclusions of the state court, and the federal appeals court followed suit. Four weeks ago, the United States Supreme Court denied review—finally bringing the 1996 habeas action to a close.

The result was the right one in the end—but it took nine years, thousands of attorney hours, and unimaginable anguish to the victim's parents and family to undue the damage caused by the original federal habeas judge.

These cases—and they are typical of my colleagues' experiences in other parts of the country—demonstrate the inherent imbalance in the exercise of federal habeas review over state criminal convictions. Federal habeas courts have great power, simply because they are last in line. But they have little responsibility, because they are so far removed in time and space from the circumstances of the crime and the subtleties of the state proceedings. Accordingly, they have small motive to act expeditiously or efficiently, to give credit to the judgments of their brethren in state courts, or to consider the needs of crime victims.

The only way that balance can be restored is by Congressional statute. H.R. 3035, the Streamlined Procedures Act, will do much to limit overreaching by federal habeas courts, while still providing an appropriate forum for criminal defendants raising legitimate constitutional challenges to their convictions. Section 2 of the bill, for example, requiring dismissal with prejudice of claims that have not been "exhausted" in state court, will help prevent another Lisa Lambert abuse, where the federal judge improperly granted relief on the basis of claims that the state courts had never had a chance to consider.

Similarly, Section 4 of the bill, concerning claims that were procedurally defaulted in state court, will address cases like Joseph Kindler, who was readily able to secure relief in federal court despite forfeiting his right to review by escaping from prison every chance he got.

Section 8, establishing time limits for federal habeas appeals, would address the indefensible delay that routinely occurs during the appellate process in cases like Mumia Abu-Jamal and William Holland. And Section 9, which effectively reactivates the special provisions for capital sentences that were first put in place by the 1995 AEDPA legislation, will provide at least a semblance of judiciousness when death penalties are challenged in federal habeas court, as in the Brian Thomas case.

Other notable provisions of the bill include Section 11, which would prohibit the kind of secret, back-door rulings that occurred in the Michael Pierce case, and Section 12, which will require federal courts to afford the same rights to victims of state crimes that are now statutorily mandated for victims of federal crimes.

These and the other sections of the Streamlined Procedures Act address distortions of the habeas litigation process that cannot be justified under the central principle of federal habeas review: comity between the state and federal judicial systems. The substance of H.R. 3035 has been endorsed by the Pennsylvania District Attorneys Association, the Attorney General of Pennsylvania, and the Pennsylvania Chiefs of Police Association. I am sure it will receive similar support in other jurisdictions. The bill merits the support of this Committee as well. Thank you.

Mr. COBLE. Thank you, Mr. Eisenberg.

Professor Harcourt, you are going to be our clean-up hitter, but I am going to ask you to suspend for a moment. We have this series of votes on the floor. And gentlemen, I hate to inconvenience you all and those in the audience, but I think it is going to take close to an hour. We have one 15-minute vote, and I am told six 5-minute votes. So if you all will just rest easy, and we will be back as soon as we can. We will momentarily be in recess.

[Whereupon, at 1:40 p.m., the Subcommittee was recessed, subject to the call of the Chair.]

[2:55 p.m.]

Mr. COBLE. Professor, you are recognized for 5 minutes.

TESTIMONY OF BERNARD E. HARCOURT, PROFESSOR OF LAW/FACULTY DIRECTOR OF ACADEMIC AFFAIRS, UNIVERSITY OF CHICAGO

Mr. HARCOURT. Thank you, Chairman Coble, Ranking Member Scott, and Members of the Committee for inviting me to comment on H.R. 3035, the "Streamlined Procedures Act of 2005." I have submitted a full statement that addresses in detail the specific problems with the provision of this bill. I have also prepared a statement. But before I begin, let me refocus our attention on what precisely we are talking about here.

H.R. 3035, the bill under consideration today, strips jurisdiction from all Federal courts to review all Federal habeas corpus claims in State death penalty cases. Now there is one precondition and there is one limited exception. The precondition is that the United States Attorney General certifies that the State provides competent counsel in State post-conviction. And the one limited exception is a claim of innocence. And I say it's extremely limited because it's only for claims of DNA evidence. It is only in cases where no reasonable fact finder would find the petitioner guilty of the offense. So with that precondition and with that limited exception, there's no more Federal habeas corpus in State death penalty cases.

In addition, the provision has a number of other provisions that are equally radical and that apply to all criminal cases, not just death penalty cases, but ordinary drug offenses, white collar crime and any other criminal case.

Now I would like to emphasize today three central problems with this bill.

First, contrary to the title of the legislation, the Streamlined Procedures Act will do nothing to streamline the Federal appeals process, but will bog down the Federal courts, actually delaying justice to victims of crime. This is a radical measure that would overturn a whole series of Supreme Court cases.

Congressman Conyers mentioned three cases earlier. When I go through the bill, I see five Supreme Court cases that are overturned by this bill: *Rhines v. Weber; Wainwright v. Sykes; Carey v. Saffold; Lindh v. Murphy;* and *Ohio Adult Parole Authority v. Woodard.* That is going to trigger spawn a huge round of Constitution litigation about Federal habeas corpus that will consume the Federal courts and the United States Supreme Court for at least a decade. It's going to complicate and delay the litigation and it's going to invite constitutional challenges. The reason very simply is that the bill strips Federal Court jurisdiction to determine many Federal issues and undercuts the Supreme Court's efforts to clear up uncertainties regarding the reform package that Congress enacted in 1996, the Antiterrorism and Effective Death Penalty Act, the AEDPA.

Now it's taken approximately a decade for the Federal courts and for the United States Supreme Court to begin to iron out what Congress did in the AEDPA and to render it somewhat functional, well understood, and applied. Just this term, just this week, we have had a number of decisions from the United States Supreme Court trying to interpret the AEDPA from 1996. It has literally taken a decade. And this legislation is going to do the same thing and provoke the same decade-long round of interpretive schedules and constitutional challenges.

Second, the Streamlined Procedures Act undermines the recent bipartisan action by Congress to address inaccuracies in the criminal justice system. I'm referring specifically to the Innocence Protection Act, which was enacted as part of the Justice for All Act, and which was a bipartisan 5-year effort that was voted 393 to 14 in this House. It passed by voice vote in the Senate before being signed by President Bush in October of 2004. The passage of the Innocence Protection Act was significant because it demonstrated the sense of Congress that we must provide additional safeguards to protect against inaccuracies and injustice in our criminal justice system, not to eliminate long-established principles concerning Federal review of criminal cases.

And it's important to note also that some of the provisions in the bill H.R. 3035 are in direct conflict with the IPA. For instance, in the IPA, a petitioner is entitled to DNA testing if it may produce new evidence that would raise, quote, "a reasonable probability of innocence." In contrast, under the SPA, the bill we're looking at today, if the Attorney General approves the State system for post-conviction representation, a petitioner can't get relief unless he establishes by clear and convincing evidence a different kind of standard, his innocence. So there are conflicts between those two bills.

Third, the Streamlined Procedures Act would increase the risk that wrongfully convicted petitioners would be executed or languish in prison. Many of the proposals in this bill would preclude claims brought by wrongfully convicted prisoners. By closing the door on the underlying Federal claims that support evidence of actual innocence, this legislation effectively closes the door on habeas corpus to actual innocent prisoners, possibly some on death row.

Now the stringent provisions of the Streamlined Procedures Act will result in serious harm to ordinary criminal defendants, especially those without lawyers who are unable to properly navigate the law.

In summing up, I would like to make this critical point clear about the legislation. Opposition to this bill does not represent opposition to the death penalty. And the two issues should not be confused here. This bill goes much further than dealing just with the death penalty. It deals with all State crimes from ordinary drug possession all the way to accounting practices, and it strikes at the very heart of the checks and balances that makes our criminal justice system unique in this country and the world.

[The prepared statement of Mr. Harcourt follows:]

PREPARED STATEMENT OF BERNARD E. HARCOURT

Statement of Bernard E. Harcourt

I would like to focus my remarks today on H.R. 3035, the "Streamlined Procedures Act of 2005," for the very simple reason that this proposed bill is radical. It seeks a radical cutting and slashing of our existing process of federal habeas corpus review of state convictions under the Anti-Terrorism and Effective Death Penalty Act reform package that Congress carefully crafted in 1996 (the "AEDPA"). This new bill would effectively gut federal habeas corpus review where states have imposed a sentence of death—in other words, in the most important habeas cases—as well as in non-capital cases. To give a simple idea of how extremely radical this proposed legislation really is, let me just point to three provisions:

(1) Section 9, titled "Capital Cases," effectively strips all federal courts of jurisdiction to consider most claims in state death penalty cases if the United States Attorney General certifies that the state from which the conviction emanated provides competent counsel to indigent capital defendants in state post-conviction proceedings. In other words, in those states in which the Attorney General certifies that counsel is provided in state post-conviction, there will likely be *no more federal habeas corpus review in death penalty cases*. Under this legislation, the federal courts will no longer have jurisdiction to ensure reliable convictions of capital murder and sentences of death. The one narrow and limited exception for claims of actual innocence comes with conditions that scarcely anyone would be able to satisfy. This is radical surgery. It would virtually abolish federal habeas corpus review for state prisoners in death penalty cases.

(2) Section 4, titled "Procedurally Defaulted Claims," eviscerates the carefully crafted standard of "cause and prejudice" that Chief Justice William Rehnquist thoughtfully and deliberately articulated in *Wainwright v. Sykes* in 1977. The Chief Justice's standard for procedurally defaulted claims represented a careful though substantial narrowing of the earlier standard of "deliberate bypass" articulated in *Fay v. Noia* in 1963. The standard for procedural default has achieved a well-recognized and well-understood level of equilibrium in the federal courts, so much so, in fact, that Congress effectively retained Chief Justice Rehnquist's standard when it adopted the AEDPA by being silent on the matter. It was well understood by all responsible reformers that the standard worked well and was being applied properly by federal courts. This proposed legislation effectively slashes this entire body of law. Again, this is radical surgery that is being proposed.

(3) Section 6, titled "Harmless Error in Sentencing," effectively eliminates federal review of any sentencing claim that a state court has found to be harmless or non-prejudicial. Again, this Section covers a large portion of sentencing claims raised in federal habeas corpus, since in reality there would be no federal habeas petition if the sentencing claims had not been found to be harmless or non-prejudicial. This section would primarily affect death penalty cases where the question typically is whether counsel rendered the effective assistance of counsel at the death sentencing phase—a two prong standard that is generally resolved on the basis of the prejudice prong with a finding of no prejudice. In effect, in a single stroke, Section 6 wipes out federal court jurisdiction to review most capital sentencing issues. This section also applies to non-capital cases.

Again, not to put too fine a point on this extremely blunt proposed legislation: This is radical surgery that is being proposed, the functional equivalent of amputating four limbs to improve the blood flow of a healthy and functioning human being. I say "healthy and functioning" because federal habeas corpus under the revised and streamlined provisions of the AEDPA are only now, finally, after a decade of federal litigation, beginning to be ironed out by the United States Supreme Court and beginning to be understood by federal District and Circuit Courts. It has, literally, taken almost ten years for the AEDPA to become functional, well-understood, and applied. This proposed legislation would not only deprive federal courts of jurisdiction to review highly meritorious claims, but would also spawn a new round of constitutional and statutory litigation that would preoccupy the federal courts for the next decade—or at least until the next wave of habeas reform.

H.R. 3035 proposes radical changes to our existing system of federal habeas corpus review under the AEDPA that would, in all likelihood, result in the execution of citizens who have been wrongly convicted and sentenced to death. This proposed legislation would virtually eliminate the ability of federal courts to determine federal issues in cases in which a state prisoner—whether facing a death sentence or serving a prison term—seeks relief by means of habeas corpus. It would overrule numerous Supreme Court cases, many of which are based on constitutional principles of federalism, separation of powers, and comity. And in the process, rather than streamlining habeas corpus, this legislation would complicate the litigation of all criminal cases, especially death penalty cases, invite massive constitutional challenges on the theory that the legislation impairs the independence of the federal courts, and delay resolution of these cases at the expense of victims and their families. The real effect of this legislation would be to bog down the federal courts with new challenges to these streamlined procedures.

To be sure, the legislation does include an exception for claims of actual innocence. However, that escape valve is far too narrow, far too limited, and far too constrained to prevent innocent persons from being executed or sent to prison. A petitioner who claims actual innocence must demonstrate that: (1) his factual predicate "could not have been previously discovered through the exercise of due diligence;" (2) the underlying facts "would be sufficient to establish by clear and convincing evidence that but for constitutional error, no reasonable factfinder would have found the applicant guilty;" *and* (3) a denial of relief on the basis of the claim would be "contrary to, or would entail an unreasonable application of, clearly established Federal law, as determined by the Supreme Court." Clearly, a genuinely innocent death row inmate could be foreclosed from raising actual innocence for a variety of reasons: The new evidence could possibly have been discovered earlier, or the evidence might not clearly and convincingly persuade every reasonable judge or jury, or it might not be unreasonable to reject the constitutional claim itself apart from any evidence of actual innocence.

The evidence necessary to demonstrate actual innocence is never born full-grown. In practically all cases of exoneration, the evidence develops gradually, in bits and pieces, over time. The evidence may start to develop by means of a claimed *Brady* violation (i.e. failure to disclose exculpatory evidence), a *Giglio* violation (i.e. failure to disclose a deal with a state witness), or the recantation of a crucial state witness. Most often, those first pieces of evidence are not one-hundred percent persuasive. Standing alone, by themselves, they are not necessarily convincing to all reasonable fact finders. But they become completely convincing over time, as the *Brady* or *Giglio* claims start unearthing more evidence of innocence, as they mature into full-blown misconduct, admissions of falsification, or discovery of new exculpating evidence. To require petitioners to prove their innocence without allowing them to litigate the underlying constitutional violations that have effectively masked their innocence is to blink reality: It is to ignore the tragic lessons that we learned about exoneration over the last two decades. It is to ignore the terrible history of exonerations of death row inmates in my home state, Illinois—where 13 death row inmates were exonerated during a period when 12 death row inmates were executed.

Well-established practice in criminal litigation confirms that proving innocence is an incremental, step-by-step process. I personally learned this the hard way in a case involving an innocent death row inmate in Alabama named Walter McMillian. Along with Bryan Stevenson, the director of the Equal Justice Initiative, we were able to ultimately prove Mr. McMillian's innocence and escort him off Alabama's death row on March 2, 1993. But we were only able to prove his innocence step by step, in increments, in bits and pieces. Like most death penalty cases, this was not a DNA exoneration. We were able to piece together overwhelming proof of innocence, starting with a recantation of the lead witness, which was then verified by multiple *Brady* violations regarding the failure to disclose the state witness's numerous pre-trial statements to doctors and law enforcement officials adamantly asserting that he was being coerced to frame an innocent man; by numerous *Giglio* violations regarding the state's failure to disclose that another state witness had been well remunerated and released from detention for his false testimony; as well as significant other evidence of innocence. The fact is, none of this evidence could have been developed and presented in federal court as one package if this legislation had been in effect—in other words, if the other constitutional violations had not been allowed to proceed. Under this proposed legislation, precluding the underlying constitutional claims will undoubtedly eviscerate genuine claims of innocence.

By closing the door to the underlying federal claims that support evidence of actual innocence, this legislation effectively closes the door of habeas corpus to actually innocent prisoners and death row inmates. And as we have seen over the course of the past decade, tragically there are innocent inmates on America's Death Row.

In what follows, I will first review the more important provisions of H.R. 3035 and discuss the implications of this radical legislative proposal. I will then consider the "actual innocence" safety valve—which is not adequately protective. I will then conclude.

I. The Sections of H.R. 3035

Section 1: Short Title

This section simply states the short title of the bill—namely, the "Streamlined Procedures Act of 2005"—but the title itself is important because it is, importantly, misleading. The short title suggests that these amendments to the AEDPA will improve the efficiency of federal habeas corpus. Nothing could be further from the truth. The fact is, this legislation will spawn a new round of constitutional litigation about federal habeas corpus that will consume the federal courts and the United States Supreme Court for a decade—or until the next round of habeas reforms, whichever comes first. This proposed legislation would actually frustrate the streamlining efforts that have been under way for nearly a decade as a result of Congress enacting a comprehensive reform program with the AEDPA in 1996. Since that time, federal courts—and especially the United States Supreme Court—have spent an inordinate amount of time, energy, and deliberation trying to iron out the confusing language in the AEDPA in an effort to make the federal habeas system operate effectively. This bill would simply churn existing Supreme Court jurisprudence and produce new litigation requiring yet more time and effort to interpret. Many of the sections of this legislation would raise significant constitutional questions about the power of Congress to restrict federal court review of habeas claims, including whether or not the bill violates the Suspension Clause of the United States Constitution. Pending death penalty and non-capital cases would be held up while the courts resolve questions about the meaning of the new law.

The fact is, several sections in this legislation—especially Sections 6 and 9, discussed below—would raise constitutional challenges on the theory that they invade the independence of the federal courts under Article III. Courts with the responsibility of decision necessarily must be entitled to address issues crucial to an appropriate judgment. Congress cannot ask them to adjudicate cases and, in the same breath, tell them what results to reach. The enactment of these provisions would invite more lawsuits challenging not only the new provisions in this bill, but also the AEDPA.

The constitutional difficulty with this proposed legislation is straightforward: The bill contemplates that federal courts would take jurisdiction of cases in order to decide whether previous state court judgments are valid, but then it would deny those courts jurisdiction to decide questions of federal law that are crucial to reaching proper results. This would deprive federal courts of their Article III authority to decide cases within their jurisdiction according to the Constitution, as well as principles of separation of powers, and it would arguably suspend the writ of habeas corpus without a justifying national emergency. These are significant constitutional claims that will preoccupy federal courts at all levels of federal habeas corpus review.

Section 2: Mixed Petitions

This second section deals with what are called "mixed petitions"—namely federal petitions that raise both claims that have been exhausted in state post-conviction proceedings and claims that have not been exhausted. Under this new provision, federal courts would be *required* to dismiss *with prejudice* unexhausted claims regardless of the merits of the claim. The section effectively withdraws all judicious discretion from the federal courts. The section also requires state prisoners—most of whom have no lawyers in state post-conviction—to press each of their federal claims in state court with special care, articulating the specific federal basis for each claim, and to explain in their federal petitions how they have complied with that mandate.

The only exceptions would be for prisoners whose claims rest on "new rules" of law that have retroactive effect or on newly discovered evidence clearly demonstrating that the prisoner did not commit the crime of which he was convicted. Even then, no exception would be allowed unless a claim is so plainly meritorious that it would be unreasonable to reject it—the actual innocence exception discussed later. It is important to note here that, since 1989, when the Supreme Court announced its current doctrine regarding "new rules," the Supreme Court has never given a new procedural rule retrospective effect. Only novel rules of substantive law, such as the prohibition on executing mentally retarded prisoners, apply to older cases. Accordingly, the only procedural claims that would fall into the exception this section allows would be claims going to factual innocence—irrespective of whether a prisoner's federal constitutional rights were violated.

What this provision does is effectively handcuff federal courts from exercising the kind of judicious discretion that is necessary to avoid miscarriages of justice in criminal cases. The federal courts use this discretion sparingly, but it is crucial to the system and to the legitimacy of criminal justice review in this country. This section would effectively overturn the Supreme Court's careful decision this Term in *Rhines v. Weber* (2005), allowing a federal district court to hold a habeas petition on its docket while a prisoner takes his claims to state court. This section would transform the exhaustion doctrine from a device that keeps federal courts from adjudicating claims before the state courts have had a chance to correct their own errors into an absolute prohibition on federal court consideration of federal claims.

Section 3: Amendments to Petitions

This third section would limit a petitioners ability to amend his federal habeas corpus petitions to only once and then only if he acts before the state files its answer. It would not allow prisoners to add new claims, unless they meet the extremely tight standards for filing second or successive habeas petitions. A provision in the AEDPA established a similar restriction in death penalty cases, but only in states that provide indigent death row inmates with competent lawyers in state post-conviction. This section would impose essentially the same limitation on amendments *across the board*—for non-capital as well as capital cases—regardless of whether the state provides counsel in state court. This too is a significant limitation to the administration of justice, especially for petitioners who may be indigent and without counsel.

Section 4: Procedurally Defaulted Claims

This fourth section is one of the most radical provisions in the proposed legislation. It would effectively strip federal courts of jurisdiction to review claims that were procedurally defaulted in state court. The federal courts would have no choice but to accept at face value a state court's decision that some state procedural rule established a procedural requirement, that the prisoner or his attorney failed to comply with that requirement, and that, in consequence, the state court declined to consider the prisoner's federal claim. In explicit language, this section also eliminates federal court jurisdiction to consider whether the petitioner's alleged procedural default in state court was attributable to his lawyer's ineffective assistance of counsel. The only exceptions, again, would be for petitioners whose claims rest on "new rules" of law that have retroactive effect or on newly discovered evidence showing that the prisoner is innocent. Under this section, accordingly, federal constitutional claims would be barred from *both* state and federal court, irrespective of their merit.

Incidentally, this section is written in an extraordinarily overbroad manner, such that it even precludes a federal court form considering a claim that *was addressed on the merits* by the state court if that court also mentioned that the petition may have committed a procedural default by failing to raise the claim properly in state court. In addition, it would deprive a federal court of jurisdiction to examine a claim that a state court was willing to review for plain error—unless the claim rests on a "new rule" of law that has retroactive effect or on newly discovered facts showing that the prisoner shouldn't have been convicted.

Congress has always left the problems associated with procedural mistakes in state court to the United States Supreme Court, which has handled those problems under the well-developed "cause and prejudice" standard established in a long line of decisions following Chief Justice Rehnquist's opinion for the Court in *Wainwright v. Sykes* (1977). This proposed change—again, a form of radical surgery—would overrule well established precedent and a large body of Supreme Court case law, and in the process trigger a whole new statutory rules that would have to be interpreted in yet another potentially large body of judicial decisions. The proposed bill opens a veritable can of worms.

Section 5: Tolling of Limitation Period

This fifth section would overrule yet another careful and recent United States Supreme Court decision, specifically *Carey v. Saffold.* In the process, the section would create a havoc of computational complexities that would bog the courts down in all kinds of litigation over filing dates, mandate dates, issuance dates, and so forth.

Under the AEDPA as it now stands, the one-year period for filing a federal petition is suspended while a "properly filed" application for state relief is "pending." If a prisoner is unsuccessful before the lowest level state court, he usually can either seek appellate review of that court's decision or start afresh with an independent application in a higher state court. Either way, there is a gap between the date he formally leaves one court and the date he begins in the next. In *Saffold,* the Court held that so long as a prisoner proceeds according to state law (meeting all the filing deadlines the state itself may establish), the federal filing period is suspended from the date the prisoner first goes to a state court until the highest state court acts.

This section, by contrast, would require a federal court to examine the state court records, compute any period of time (however brief) when a prisoner was not formally before some state court, and charge that time against the one-year federal filing period.

In addition, this section would also mandate that if an application for relief in state court is to suspend the filing period for a federal habeas corpus petition, it must contain alleged violations of the prisoner's federal rights. Under existing AEDPA law, a petition tolls the time for filing a federal habeas if it contains only claims based on state law. This makes entire sense: if the state courts find a state-law claim meritorious and grant relief on that basis, there will be no need for federal courts to become involved at all. This section would frustrate that means of reducing the number of federal habeas petitions.

Finally, this section would forbid federal courts to relax the one-year filing period on equitable grounds—when there are extremely good reasons why a prisoner was unable to get to federal court within one year. All federal courts now allow for that possibility, though they rarely actually give prisoners more time. This section would eliminate that authority. Here again, the proposed legislation does violence to the important interest that federal courts have in equitable discretion, administered responsibly.

Section 6: Harmless Error in Sentencing

This section would strip federal courts of jurisdiction to entertain most claims regarding a sentence if a state court found any constitutional error that occurred to be "harmless" or "not prejudicial." The only exceptions would be for prisoners who demonstrate that the violations they suffered were "structural." (By definition, structural claims cannot *be* "harmless." And in any event, very, very few errors are "structural" in the necessary sense, so the exception for structural error cases is inconsequential).

Sentencing claims are by no means frivolous, nor do they simply clog up the federal dockets. In death penalty cases, they often raise the most important issues to be resolved. And in sentencing guideline cases, as demonstrated recently in the Supreme Court's decisions in *Apprendi v. New Jersey* and *Booker v. United States,* they often raise crucial issues of constitutional dimension. This section would carve out an enormous share of the federal courts' jurisdiction to adjudicate important sentencing issues, especially in capital cases. Nothing in this section would allow a federal court to examine whether a state court correctly determined that a trial error was "not prejudicial." So the federal court would be expected to resolve a constitutional case without the authority to determine independently the crucial federal issue. This would invite constitutional challenges for invading federal court independence.

Section 7: Unified Review Standard

This seventh section would make the provisions in AEDPA applicable to cases that were already pending on the date that Act became law. Thus it would overturn still another careful Supreme Court decision, *Lindh v. Murphy*, which construed AEDPA not to extend some of its key provisions to pending cases. The decision in *Lindh* not only respected Congress' wishes, but also eased the transition from prior law to the new AEDPA regime. Extending AEDPA to those cases would invite arguments about whether Congress genuinely means to impose new legal consequences on events in the past and, if so, whether changing the rules of the game retroactively is constitutional. Both arguments would, of course, trigger yet more litigation.

Section 8: Appeals

This section would establish new timetables for federal courts to follow in processing appeals in habeas cases. AEDPA contains similar timetables—but only for death penalty cases and then only for cases arising from states that give something in return, namely counsel for indigents in state post-conviction proceedings.

This long, intricate, and confusing section does not address a genuine problem. There is no good evidence that federal appellate courts fail to handle habeas appeals expeditiously. The most likely consequence of this section is that the federal courts would have to lay aside ordinary civil and criminal cases in order to rush habeas corpus cases to judgment, which may compromise the quality of the courts' work—raising yet another basis for a constitutional challenge.

Section 9: Capital Cases

This section, again, is perhaps the most radical one in the proposed bill. It would strip federal courts of jurisdiction to consider most claims (going either to a conviction or to a sentence) in death penalty cases arising from states that supply competent counsel to indigents in state post-conviction proceedings. The jurisdictional prohibition would operate even with respect to claims the state courts failed to address. The only exceptions would be for prisoners who advance claims based on retroactive "new rules" and those who offer newly discovered evidence clearly demonstrating their actual innocence. This is one of the most far-reaching attacks on federal jurisdiction in habeas corpus in recent history.

Under current AEDPA law, a state can trigger a special set of more advantageous (to the state) procedural rules for federal habeas proceedings if the state establishes an effective system for providing competent counsel to indigents in state post-conviction proceedings. Federal courts determine whether a state's scheme for supplying counsel meets the statutory criteria. This is the so-called "opt in" feature of AEDPA. A state *gets* something (advantageous procedural rules in federal court) in exchange for *doing* something (providing good lawyers to indigents in state proceedings). This section would change both ends of that *quid pro quo* equation. First, and most importantly, the state would no longer *need* favorable procedural rules in federal court, because they would get an absolute jurisdictional prohibition on federal court consideration of most federal claims. Second, states would no longer have to satisfy federal courts that their systems for providing counsel in state proceedings are adequate, because the authority to approve state schemes would be transferred to the United States Attorney General. (The Court of Appeals for the District of Columbia would have exclusive jurisdiction to review his or her decisions, but only for an abuse of discretion).

Here too, by placing the authority to decide these matters with the Attorney General—a law enforcement official—the proposed legislation disturbs the existing allocation and separation of powers, and raises another set of potential issues for extended litigation.

Section 10: Clemency and Pardon Decision

This section would strip federal courts of jurisdiction to entertain federal claims arising in clemency and pardon cases. Its extremely broad language would overrule *Ohio Adult Parole Authority v. Woodard* (1998), in which the Supreme Court held in a case brought under Section 1983 that an inmate was entitled to assert the claim that the clemency procedures of a particular state violate minimal standards of due process under the federal constitution. This provision seems like a gratuitous effort to prevent federal review of established due process rights.

Section 11: Ex Parte Funding Requests

This section would bar federal judges entertaining habeas petitions from handling requests for financial support from attorneys representing petitioners. It would shift that responsibility to other judges. It would also usually require the proceedings on such a request—as well as the amounts allowed—to be public.

Section 14: Application to Pending Cases

This section would make the proposed legislation applicable to already pending federal habeas corpus cases. This section too, like Section 7, would trigger massive litigation over whether the United States Constitution allows Congress to attach legal consequences to events in the past.

The other two sections, 12 and 13, are less controversial. Section 12, "Crime Victims' Rights," merely extends the essentials of the Crime Victims' Rights Act (applicable to federal criminal proceedings) to habeas corpus cases. It would entitle victims to attend habeas hearings and to be notified of "developments" in habeas proceedings. Section 13, "Technical Corrections," merely authorizes district judges to allow prisoners to appeal in habeas corpus cases. It conforms to current practice.

II. Actual Innocence

It has been suggested that this bill preserves access to the federal courts in cases in which state prisoners may actually be innocent. That is not so. This bill would strip federal courts of jurisdiction to determine a host of federal issues in capital and non-capital cases alike, without any effective safety valve for prisoners who may have been erroneously convicted. The provisions that are supposed to protect actually innocent people come with conditions that scarcely anyone would be able to satisfy. There are numerous examples:

Section 2 would instruct a federal court to dismiss any claim that has not previously been presented to the state courts without giving the prisoner the opportunity to return to state court for further consideration. There are exceptions, but they are extremely limited. As noted earlier, a petitioner who claims actual innocence must demonstrate that: (1) his factual predicate "could not have been previously discovered through the exercise of due diligence;" (2) the underlying facts "would be sufficient to establish by clear and convincing evidence that but for constitutional error, no reasonable factfinder would have found the applicant guilty;" *and* (3) a denial of relief on the basis of the claim would be "contrary to, or would entail an unreasonable application of, clearly established Federal law, as determined by the Supreme Court." Clearly, a genuinely innocent death row inmate could be foreclosed from raising actual innocence for a variety of reasons.

Section 4 would strip a federal court of jurisdiction to entertain a claim the state courts declined to consider on the basis of some procedural error committed by the prisoner or his lawyer in state court. Again, there are exceptions. But they are the same exceptions. So, again, a prisoner who has newly discovered evidence of actual innocence might be turned away from federal court on the ground that the evidence might have been found earlier, that it doesn't clearly and convincingly demonstrate actual innocence to every reasonable person, or that the claim the state courts refused to consider might be rejected without acting unreasonably.

Section 9 would strip a federal court of jurisdiction to consider *any* claim advanced by a prisoner under sentence of death—if the Attorney General has certified that a state's system for providing counsel to prisoners in state post-conviction proceedings is adequate. Again, only similar narrow exceptions are allowed. A prisoner whose life is at stake would have to prove both that the newly discovered evidence couldn't have been located earlier and that the new facts would clearly and convincingly satisfy any reasonable person that the prisoner is not guilty.

III. Conclusion

In closing, I should emphasize that in these remarks that I have set aside H.R. 3060, the "Terrorist Death Penalty Enhancement Act," because the latter proposed bill is essentially unrelated to the radical surgery proposed in H.R. 3035. Certainly, all important prosecutions of terrorists will proceed through military or federal criminal prosecution, and not in state courts. As a result, the proposed changes in H.R. 3035, which address federal review of *state* cases, do not fall within the ambit of anti-terrorism legislation.

In sum, H.R. 3035 is radical, jurisdiction-stripping legislation that would unnecessarily churn what is gradually becoming well-settled AEDPA jurisprudence. It should be avoided.

Mr. COBLE. Thank you, Professor. And I thank each of the panelists. As I told you previously, we impose the 5-minute rule against us as well, so if you could keep your responses as terse as possible. And I suspect we will have a second round because of the interest that this matter has generated.

Mr. Marquis, in your testimony you attach a critique of the Death Penalty Information Center list of persons freed from death row. Describe in general what the analysis shows. How does the analysis of the DPIC position further the debate on the death penalty in America? And what is meant by the term "false exonerations?"

Mr. MARQUIS. That summary needs to be credited to Ward Campbell, who is the supervising assistant attorney general in California who has been working on it for years. And the Death Penalty Information Center is a very neutral sounding group that is an anti-death penalty group that puts out a list, and it is the one that's generally acknowledged, with 115 names of people supposedly exonerated. What Ward did is go through every single case to see whether or not there really was evidence of innocence. And what it turns up is that in a majority, if not a very large number of the cases, that there is very little evidence of actual innocence. And that in fact, many other cases, there is considerable evidence of guilt.

My personal favorite is a guy named Jay Smith from Pennsylvania, who was off death row and his case thrown out. He then sues the Pennsylvania State Police. And the Third Circuit Court of Appeals, not known for its conservatism, throws out his case and says, even if the prosecutor misconducted himself, we are still convinced you are guilty. It goes to the issue I spoke of, using the word "innocent" and "exonerated" when you are talking about people really has to be done very carefully. And Mr. Scott talked about people exonerated by DNA. We need to know how many that is. It's 12 people.

Mr. COBLE. Mr. Eisenberg, in Professor Harcourt's testimony, he asserted that the Streamlined Procedures Act would complicate the litigation of all criminal cases, especially death penalty cases, and delay resolution of these cases at the expense of victims and their families. Do you agree with this assessment?

Mr. EISENBERG. Mr. Chairman, I am heartened that we recognize that this delay is a concern because of the difficulties it causes for victims and their families. I wish that more Federal courts were cognizant of that. It's certainly not true that this bill will delay things, because in the absence of this bill we face endless delay. Nothing has been resolved. Nothing has been ended. The delays that we face are only growing, because it's not a question of the Supreme Court cleaning up this or that little area of law.

I argued in the Supreme Court just a few months ago—and again I did last year, and we expect to see more cases go there in the future, whether or not the law is changed—we are going to be facing lengthy rounds of litigation in the lower courts that then apply those Supreme Court cases. And judges who want to use those cases, however many precedents there are, in order to drag things out in the lower courts, they are going to be able to do that no matter what the statute is. That is the lesson of the AEDPA.

Mr. COBLE. Mr. Sabin, in addition to the provisions contained in this bill, are there any additional death penalty legislative recommendations that the Justice Department would like for our Committee to consider?

Mr. SABIN. The answer is yes, Mr. Chairman. I have had a chance to discuss with some of the experts at the Justice Department. For example, under *Atkins v. Virginia,* where the Supreme Court held that the execution of a mentally retarded offender would violate the eighth amendment, we would recommend that a procedure be put into place legislatively to determine whether a capital defendant's mental capacity is such that a death sentence would be appropriate or would be foreclosed under the *Atkins* decision. There are certain notice of intent provisions that are required to be filed a reasonable time before trial, and we believe that a statutory clarification regarding that notice of intent, based upon a Fourth Circuit case, would be helpful.

There is also certain clarification regarding the meaning of specific statutory aggravating factors; for example, the pecuniary gain aggravating factor, that I think legislation would be helpful. And the Justice Department on those and other matters would work with the Committee to make sure that the Committee understood the Justice Department's recommendations, if appropriate, are enacted.

Mr. COBLE. Have you all conveyed that information to our Committee or Subcommittee?

Mr. SABIN. I believe the discussions have occurred. I can follow up and make sure that some of those are specifically forwarded to the Subcommittee.

Mr. COBLE. I thank you, sir. My 5 minutes have expired, but I didn't see the red light. But I will recognize the distinguished gentleman from Michigan, Mr. Conyers, for 5 minutes.

Mr. CONYERS. Thank you very much, Mr. Chairman. We seem to have three witnesses that are, I think, in agreement with each other. So I turn to Professor Harcourt. Will we face endless delay if we don't enact this—one of these two measures that are before us? Could you give us your views on that, sir?

Mr. HARCOURT. We are in the process of having ironed out basically the provisions of the AEDPA. The Supreme Court has resolved most of the questions that are outstanding. And at this point, the Federal death penalty and ordinary criminal cases that are going through habeas corpus should be proceeding at a much more rapid pace as a result of the AEDPA. It appears that there are, in fact, less cases that are being overturned by Federal courts as a result of the reforms that—the package of reforms that were passed in 1996. And so I think it's pretty clear there is less and less delay as a result of that reform.

Mr. CONYERS. Thank you very much. Now let's get back to the constant debate that will probably not be resolved in this Subcommittee today. But is the death penalty a deterrent from your studies?

Mr. HARCOURT. Well, on the question of deterrence, I think it's far too early to make any conclusions about the validity of the studies, of the new econometric studies.

Mr. CONYERS. Sorry to hear that, because I had thought I was able to say that there is no deterrent effect.

Mr. HARCOURT. The new studies that have come out from the economists, et cetera, are kind of divided on the issue of deterrence. There are some that suggest there is a deterrent effect to the death penalty and there are others that suggest that if you cut it in different ways, there isn't a deterrent effect to the death penalty and, in fact, there is a brutalizing effect to executions. We have had cycles of social science debates about issues such as deterrence. In the 1970's, there was significant debate over the Ehrlich study, which resulted in the National Academy of Science report that essentially said there is no evidence of deterrence.

What we have right now is a new series of studies. And frankly, the honest truth is that it is much too early to form any conclusions based on those studies. The death penalty is a highly ideological and political debate and that extends into the social sciences.

Mr. CONYERS. Counsel—our counsel, Bobby Vassar, has handed me a letter from assistant Federal Defender John Rhodes, sent to him this month from Montana, Federal Defenders of Montana, in which I will read the operative sentence: The 159 cases to which I referred were those in which post-conviction DNA testing has yielded conclusive proof of innocence. Of these 159 people, 14 have been sentenced to death, 39 to life imprisonment, and others to various terms.

And I was wondering, does that comport with your understanding of how these statistics are falling out?

Mr. HARCOURT. Yes, Congressman Conyers. My number is 156. I have 156 DNA exonerations around the country. 156. We are talking about proof based on DNA that this wasn't the right person. Of those, my numbers were 12 death penalty DNA exonerations. I think you mentioned 14. We might be off by a year or so. I have approximately 12 death penalty DNA exonerations. The important point to understand here, of course, is in the exoneration context, you have to distinguish DNA exonerations from non-DNA exonerations. And when you don't have DNA exonerating someone, then it's practically impossible to get everybody on board to agree that the person was actually innocent. There are going to be very few cases where there isn't—there was evidence that resulted in a conviction originally and there is going to be recantation, Brady evidence that reveals new suspects, et cetera. But those are the difficult cases where, in fact, there is proof beyond a reasonable doubt of innocence. But there is going to be possibly lingering doubt, particularly like someone like Mr. Marquis. If you look at the list, the ones that are going to be challenged are the ones where there isn't a clear case of DNA evidence, but you are going to see that actually beyond a reasonable doubt that there's evidence in the case.

I represented someone myself who was innocent. It wasn't a DNA case. And I can tell you, I sat there with the two investigators from the Alabama Bureau of Investigation and we were trying to resolve, after we had proven his innocence to their satisfaction, were trying to resolve who had committed this crime. I had the ABI with me working on this case. I can assure you there are still people who are going to have questions about that case because there wasn't DNA.

Mr. COBLE. If you could wrap up so we can move along. The gentleman's time has expired.

Mr. HARCOURT. If you look at the list, you need to go through them case by case. In the case of Ronnie Burrell, it suggests there wasn't evidence. In fact, the motion that the prosecutor filed in that case said there was a total lack of credible evidence linking Graham and/or Burrell to the crime. So it's always when there isn't DNA evidence, there's always a way to say that it's not a case of innocence. But we have had over 160 of those cases as well.

Mr. CONYERS. Thank you, Chairman Coble, for your unusual generosity.

Mr. COBLE. Thank you, Mr. Conyers. I appreciate that.

In order of appearance, the gentleman from California, Mr. Lungren, is recognized for 5 minutes.

Mr. LUNGREN. Thank you, Mr. Chairman, for your customary courtesy. And——

Mr. COBLE. And I thank you for that.

Mr. LUNGREN. I was Attorney General for 8 years. We did as much habeas corpus as any office in the country would. Ward Campbell worked for me for 8 years. I hope we put this in proper context.

The suggestion has been made that somehow habeas corpus is the only way we protect defendants' rights. Capital cases, you extend more rights to the defendant than any other type of case you've got. You have bifurcated trials. You have to prove guilt or innocence. Then you go to the sentence. That sentence can be overturned by the judge. At least in California, you have immediate appeal, combined appeal, both direct appeal and habeas to the Supreme Court automatically. Whether the defendant wants it or not, it is done.

Then you go into the Federal system. And let us remember what we are talking about. As Chief Justice Rehnquist once said in a dissent, the trial should be the main event unless we are willing to give up the trial by jury as the essence of our criminal justice system. Frankly, the Federal habeas corpus is the most removed process that comes in after the fact. By and large, they don't have an opportunity to see the witnesses to judge their demeanor to see whether or not they are credible.

And I never could understand why folks believe that when a particular judge who happened to be sitting on a Federal District Court in Los Angeles, named Judge Lucas, became the chief justice of the California Supreme Court, suddenly he lost all wisdom and direction because he no longer dressed in a Federal Court but now dressed in the California Supreme Court.

Carol Fornoff testified before this Subcommittee that her 13-year-old daughter was murdered in 1984 and the last State court appeal was in 1992. The killer filed his first habeas petition in U.S. District Court, where it remained for 7 years before it was dismissed. Then the Ninth Circuit sent the case back to the district court for more hearings, where it remains today. Someone—Professor Harcourt mentioned the brutalizing effect of this. What about the brutalizing effect on the families? The Supreme Court told us in the Turpin case that it was up to Congress to write the procedures for habeas corpus and to make any changes. They invited the Congress to look at it and make changes. Contrary to any suggestion that this is out of our area of expertise, I would cite the Turpin case which recognized it's exactly in there.

I don't know about all the studies you are talking about. I can talk about a case that I argued before the United States Supreme Court. It was called the Sandoval case and involved a murderer who killed four people, two in a gang-related incident, and then later on two people who had overheard what he talked about, who were going to be witnesses, and he killed them. We won the case in the Supreme Court. It went back. And, ultimately, the death penalty was set aside for other reasons. It had nothing to do with exoneration. The guy killed four people. Four people.

I guess my question, Mr. Eisenberg, to you would be, there has been a suggestion we don't need this. There has been the suggestion that you know, if we do this, the courts are going to screw it up again and going to take time to interpret it. The suggestion is that we in Congress ought to tie our hands and not do anything because it's going to add more delay. I know the Ninth Circuit. That is one of the reasons I introduced this bill.

The Ninth Circuit, despite what we did in 1996—and my office wrote the language which was adopted by the Congress at that time—the Ninth Circuit has managed to, in exhaustion cases and procedural default cases, to get around what I think was the intent of the law to have these interminable delays. So I am familiar with the Ninth Circuit.

Could you tell me in your experience, even though we passed that law in 1996 to try and take care of that, why would we need something such as suggested in the bill?

Mr. EISENBERG. Because there were some judges, Congressman, who didn't like what was in that bill. I'm sure they won't like what is in this one. It is the job of the Congress to channel the law in the direction you think it ought to go.

Procedural default, for example, well established concept. We have thrown it around. It's a habeas term. What a Federal judge in my neck of the woods does with it is to say, well, there was a State procedural default where the defendant didn't comply with some rulings in State court, but I don't like that rule so I'm going to call it inadequate or insufficient in some way, and then I get to ignore—and therefore I get to ignore what the State court did, and I get to make my own decision about the legal questions here. And that kind of litigation sounds simple describing it. That kind of litigation takes years in my part of the country and from my discussion with others.

The same is true around the United States. It is not a question of whether the concept can be simply uncontroversial, described between habeas lawyers. It is a question of what the courts then do with that in order to apply it in particular cases. And however well established the concept is, if the court wants to use it as a means of delay and as a means of getting around a State court, it can. If Congress takes that away, that has a positive impact.

Mr. LUNGREN. Sounds like a war of attrition.

Mr. COBLE. Gentleman's time has expired.

After we adjourn this hearing, we are planning to mark up the Secure Access to Justice and Court Protection Act of 2005. So if you all could remain while we do that, I would be appreciative.

The distinguished gentleman from Massachusetts. And I want to say to him that prior to your arrival, I spoke favorably about your work on the DNA legislation the last session. You, and Chairman Sensenbrenner was involved, as was Mr. Scott and I. Good work, and I'm pleased to recognize you.

Mr. DELAHUNT. Thank you very much, Mr. Chairman. I would be interested in whether Mr. Sabin, Mr. Marquis, and I can't see that far, Mr. Eisenberg. You are familiar with the Justice for All Act?

Mr. SABIN. Yes, sir. Generally.

Mr. DELAHUNT. Did you support it?

Mr. SABIN. Personally, I didn't have a chance to weigh in. Justice Department supported it, and we are implementing the victim's provision.

Mr. MARQUIS. I am very familiar with it. And the National District Attorneys Association supported most of the parts.

Mr. DELAHUNT. I am speaking about yourself.

Mr. MARQUIS. Senator Smith was one of the cosponsors.

Mr. DELAHUNT. I'm asking about Marquis, not about Smith.

Mr. MARQUIS. I had some problems about some of the issues about when you describe innocence. But for the most part, yes.

Mr. EISENBERG. Congressman, what we did in Pennsylvania is actually go ahead and draft our own before the Federal version was passed. I participated in the drafting of that. Much of it was modeled on the legislation that was originally introduced in the Congress, and I'm very glad we passed that in the States. In fact, while discussions were going on in Washington, many States passed their own DNA legislation.

Mr. DELAHUNT. I noted that. And I applaud the States for their efforts.

Let me just say this, Mr. Chairman. This is a very—I'm referring to the Streamlined Procedures Act of 2005, offered by my good friend and someone who I have profound respect for from California. But I do have very serious concerns about this.

I guess I agree with Senator Specter who posed a question, why the rush, particularly when this week it was announced that there be a case in the fall to determine whether there is a constitutional right to stop an execution based upon a claim of innocence. And also this week, the Supreme Court ruled the competency of legal counsel is perhaps the most significant unresolved death penalty issue.

But I would hope, Mr. Chairman, that we could have a series of hearings on discrete issues surrounding the Streamlined Procedures Act, focusing in on the issues of harmless error, exhaustion issues, et cetera, because this is a dramatic departure from the current status of the law.

I'm not going to belabor the point. I think one point that really has to be stressed, you know, people—there are a few people that are probably watching these proceedings, and the reality is—and it sounds simple, of course, to the panel—what we are talking about are people who are incarcerated. These people are not out on the street wreaking mayhem on the community at large. So I think to assuage any unfounded concerns that the American people might have in terms of when they listen to our Subcommittees and your answers, should be reassured about that.

Mr. LUNGREN. Would the gentleman yield?

Mr. DELAHUNT. Sure.

Mr. LUNGREN. I can give examples of people who were the subject of habeas corpus cases with death penalties or life imprisonment in California who did commit murders while in prison. They might not have been on the street; we did see that.

Mr. DELAHUNT. I happen to have—when I was a State prosecutor, I had the major penal institutions in my jurisdiction, and we obviously had a problem with homicides within our correctional facilities. But I think there's another point, too, that we have to be cognizant of, is that there are maybe 12, 13 DNA exonerations in capital cases.

But as Professor Harcourt—I mean, how many cases are there when DNA is unavailable, 80 percent, 85 percent? It's in that neighborhood. You are all seasoned prosecutors. I think what we learned from the advent of DNA is it has given us a window into exactly what the Supreme Court is saying. The great unresolved issue is competency of counsel. And yes, the States have made progress. But I daresay anybody who has tried a lot of felony cases in a State court is aware of situations where it was clear during the course of the trial that counsel for the defendant just didn't have it. Just didn't have it.

And I think we've all been—at least my experience has been, I indicted individuals and charged them with serious crimes, and subsequently found out that they, in fact, were innocent in very real terms.

You know, what sets the United States apart from other democracies, even, is the fact that it is the main event—I think I heard that before, maybe it was from Mr. Lungren. It's not the trial. The main event really is the search for the truth. The search for the truth. And if there is doubt and if there are grounds where a habeas petition will lie, it's important for us to recognize that. That's just some observations that I would make.

And Mr. Marquis, I always found it interesting that in those jurisdictions, those States that did not have—noncapital States, their incidents of violence, often homicide rates were significantly lower.

Mr. COBLE. The gentleman's time has expired, but you may answer the question.

Mr. MARQUIS. With all due respect, Mr. Delahunt, I don't think that's actually correct. The two jurisdictions that come to mind are Michigan and the District of Columbia, none of which have capital punishment and both of which, Detroit and the District, have a terrible murder rate. I don't think there is a direct correlation. But this goes to the issue of deterrence. And there is a substantial body of study that shows differently.

Mr. DELAHUNT. It is my understanding—and we can exchange correspondence on this—that of the 12 or 13 noncapital cases, their incidence of violence, their rate of violent crime is less than those States that impose the death penalty. But we can have that conversation via correspondence. But that has always been a problem that I have had. And in fact, I think I mentioned that once to my friend from Texas, Mr. Gohmert, who will have a reply.

Mr. COBLE. Information for all of you. The record will remain open for seven days.

The distinguished gentleman from Florida will be recognized for 5 minutes, Mr. Feeney.

Mr. FEENEY. Thank you, Mr. Chairman. And as the gentleman from Massachusetts indicated, the search for truth is something we are all interested in, but hopefully the search for truth eventually has some finality to it.

One of the problems with the death penalty is the extremely lengthy and collateral processes that go on forever. Professor Harcourt testified that it's his hunch that based on the last 10 years or so of jurisprudence, that the tremendous delays are going to be less and less. But as I look at Justice Department's statistics going back to 1984, the average time between sentence and execution was about 73 months. As of 2003, that had almost doubled to 132 months.

And for Mr. Eisenberg and for Mr. Sabin, have you seen any dramatic change in the length of time between sentence and execution in the last several years?

Mr. EISENBERG. I will begin, Congressman.

Yes, it's getting longer. And as far as I can tell, the largest limiting factor is the length of life of the defendant. In my State, for example, we have had three defendants who waived their appeals and were executed, but we have had 15 who died of natural causes on death row. Their cases came to an end. But that seems to be the only way that contested capital cases come to an end in some areas of the country is when the defendant on death row dies of natural causes. Otherwise, the delays are increasing, and certainly nothing about any resolution of any questions under the AEDPA is shortening the time.

Mr. FEENEY. Mr. Sabin?

Mr. SABIN. I can't speak to specific numbers, Mr. Feeney. But as a general proposition, the point that Mr. Lungren made for closure for victims, that the process would extend on unnecessarily. And that if an injustice has occurred, I would think the offender would want that to be resolved sooner rather than later, so that the streamlining of the process, with appropriate review, would be in the interest of all.

Mr. FEENEY. Mr. Eisenberg, very quickly, you indicate that of the 20 cases in the last decade from Pennsylvania to go to a Federal court in habeas, 19 were tossed out and only 1 was upheld?

Mr. EISENBERG. It is roughly along those lines, Congressman. And that's not to say that no cases have been reversed by the State courts. On the contrary, many cases have been reversed by the State courts, perhaps more than the number that have finally reached ultimate decisions in the Federal courts.

Our State courts are extremely vigilant in reviewing death penalty cases, and many of those cases have been reversed, not even having to go up to the State Supreme Court, but by lower level State judges. Even cases that clear that complete hurdle of 10 or 20 years of litigation in State court and then get to Federal court are certainly going to be thrown out as well. We just don't have a realistic process.

Mr. FEENEY. Ninety-five percent of the time, the judge, the jury, and the entire State appellate process is simply tossed out on habeas by the Federal Court.

Mr. Marquis, if you would summarize the econometric deterrence studies that you talked about. And by the way, maybe you ought to mention, theoretically deterrence may work; but if it's going to take us 15 years before we have an execution of a sentence, there may be some diminishment of the potential deterrent effect of a death penalty; that this bill would bring back some real deterrence. And I would leave it with that.

I would like to get into the constitutional issue that has not been addressed. There is nothing in the Constitution that guarantees a collateral Federal right of habeas, which nobody has mentioned. But Mr. Marquis, I would let you finish.

Mr. MARQUIS. Yes, the studies. I think one of the other Congressmen mentioned—I'm sorry, Professor Harcourt—there is a whole cluster that have come up in the last 5 years; one from Emory University, another from the University of Houston, University of Colorado. They're mostly by economists and academics. And mostly all of the people that do the studies are opposed to the death penalty, and they studied whether or not there was deterrent from actual executions. Whether moratoriums or pardons have an effect on murders. And all of the studies, literally all of them thus far, show a significant deterrence.

And to put it in a very real sense, because I have been accused by defense experts of being too concrete a thinker, 17 murders are deterred, plus or minus 7, for every death penalty that is imposed in the United States. That's very real to me.

Mr. FEENEY. I still have a little bit of time.

The constitutional issue, Mr. Eisenberg. Anything in our Constitution guarantee any collateral, additional right of habeas corpus in Federal court?

Mr. EISENBERG. No, Congressman. The words appear—the words "habeas corpus" appear in the Constitution, but they never contemplated anything like the 10 and 20 years' worth of appeals that we're talking about. There weren't even 2 years of appeals when those words were put into the Constitution, and in some cases no appeals, you had a trial. That was the main event because it was the only event. And I think that—it is inconceivable that any founder or any lawyer in the early days of this Republic would have imagined that appeals in criminal cases could go from court to court to court and take decades long.

Mr. COBLE. The gentleman's time has expired.

The distinguished gentleman from Virginia, Mr. Scott, is recognized for 5 minutes.

Mr. SCOTT. Thank you very much.

Mr. Marquis, you indicated that one death penalty saves 18 murders; is that from the Shepherd study?

Mr. MARQUIS. Yes, it is. The main author of the study—sorry, I can't pronounce the person's name; but yes, it's that study.

Mr. SCOTT. Did Professor Shepherd review her conclusions and conclude after that, that in the 27 States in which one execution occurred during the sample period, capital punishment, in her judgment, deterred murder in six States and increased murder in 13 States and had no effect in the others? Is that a subsequent finding of hers?

Mr. MARQUIS. My understanding of what happened is that there was a blizzard of criticism of the study, and that—the argument was made that they were concentrating too much on States that had high execution rates, and if you took them out, that the rate would in fact decrease. So, I'm not sure if that answers your question.

Mr. SCOTT. Okay. In twice as many States, the murder rate went up than went down because of the death penalty.

Mr. Sabin, one of the—I'm going back and forth on these bills, and I didn't separate these questions by bill, but one of the bills has a death penalty for cases in which death does not occur.

Mr. SABIN. A grave risk of death, but not death under——

Mr. SCOTT. Has the constitutionality of the death penalty when a death does not occur—has the Supreme Court ruled on that?

Mr. SABIN. I don't believe the Supreme Court has ruled, but it's equally applicable in treason and espionage cases under the statutory provisions presently in place.

Mr. SCOTT. And death penalty, without a death occurring, is constitutional in those cases?

Mr. SABIN. I don't know if there has been a specific Supreme Court case that has addressed it in the treason or espionage case. But the theory behind the legislation, as I understand it in section 104 of H.R. 3060, is that theory, sir.

Mr. SCOTT. You have a retroactive application of the procedure. Are there cases pre-1994 for which this death penalty may apply?

Mr. SABIN. If you're referring to the quote-unquote "Safarini fix" under section 103, the answer is yes, sir. There are a number of terrorism cases that have been charged where there are defendants under indictment, that it would directly affect where United States citizens were killed.

Mr. SCOTT. You have people under indictment today that are not subject to the death penalty, and if we pass this bill, on a pending case we will allow the death penalty.

Mr. SABIN. No, sir. In 1974 the Antihijacking Act was passed; in 1994 the Federal Death Penalty Act was passed. There were specific death penalty procedures during the time period of 1974 to 1994, but in the passage of the Act in 1994, Congress did not articulate, as interpreted by the district court judge in the District of Columbia, that those provisions specifically apply and were not extinguished with the passage of the new legislation.

Mr. SCOTT. I understand the procedural; the procedural, you can do it. But I just want to know the effect of the legislation. You have people under indictment today that you cannot impose the death penalty on.

Mr. SABIN. As the district court decision was found, yes.

Mr. SCOTT. Well, you have people under indictment today that are not subject to the death penalty. If we pass this bill, you will be able to subject them to the death penalty.

Mr. SABIN. Correct.

Mr. SCOTT. Pending cases.

Mr. SABIN. Yes.

Mr. SCOTT. In the middle of the case.

Mr. SABIN. No. They're under indictment. They're either in—fugitives from justice that are not in United States custody, or they have been apprehended and are serving a sentence in a foreign country, that the United States has sought to obtain the custody of them in order to process——

Mr. SCOTT. Now, I just want to make sure we know what we've got before us. We have defendants in pending cases that are not subject to the death penalty, and we will pass legislation that would subject them to the death penalty. That may not technically be a violation of ex post facto because it's procedural, but procedural and substantive—I think it would be substantive to the ones it applied to.

Mr. SABIN. I understand your point, sir. But the point was that I believe Congress had unequivocally, and the executive branch and congressional leaders had said that those individuals were subject to the death penalty during that period of 74 to 94, so they were clearly on notice. It's not like we're changing the rules after the offense has been committed.

Mr. SCOTT. Well, if we don't pass this bill, they won't be subject to the death penalty; is that——

Mr. SABIN. District court in the District of Columbia has interpreted congressional inaction or silence in 1994 by not incorporating those provisions, such that we would not be able to seek the death penalty.

Mr. SCOTT. Was that case appealed? Is that a final judgment?

Mr. SABIN. He pled guilty to three life terms, plus 25 years, and is serving that now in a Federal penitentiary.

Mr. SCOTT. And the decision of the district court was not appealed?

Mr. SABIN. Correct.

Mr. SCOTT. So that's the only place that's been ruled.

Mr. SABIN. Correct.

Mr. SCOTT. So in other cases, you could go try for the death penalty and see what happens.

Mr. SABIN. We could. We're seeking congressional explicit recognition of that fact—which we believe Congress had previously done—but just to make sure that it is done——

Mr. SCOTT. You're seeking your own alternative court of appeals. Okay.

Mr. COBLE. The gentleman's time has expired.

We have been joined by the gentlelady from Texas. Good to have you with us, Ms. Jackson Lee. In order of appearance, the distinguished gentleman from Texas, Mr. Gohmert.

Mr. GOHMERT. Thank you, Mr. Chairman. Thank you, witnesses——

Mr. COBLE. Would the gentleman suspend? Were you here earlier, Mr. Chabot?

Mr. CHABOT. I was. But I will defer.

Mr. COBLE. If you were here earlier, that's my mistake; but I recognize the distinguished gentleman from Ohio, Mr. Chabot.

Mr. GOHMERT. I appreciated being recognized.

Mr. CHABOT. But he was a judge, I was just a lowly trial lawyer.

Mr. COBLE. And I will get to the Texan subsequently.

Mr. CHABOT. Okay. I want to first thank the Chairman for his leadership in this area. I want to thank the witnesses. I think we've had really excellent witnesses here today. I also want to thank Congressman Lungren for introducing H.R. 3035, which attempts to streamline the procedures relative to death penalty cases.

As a longtime advocate for victims rights, I've been very disturbed by the length of time that it takes for a lawfully convicted person to go from sentencing to execution in this country. The average length of time between sentencing and execution has risen from 74 months, or 6 years and 2 months in 1984, to a high of 143 months, or just shy of 12 years in 1999. And as we know, 20 years is not that rare a case in this country nowadays.

Why does it take so long for these murderers to meet their fate? All too often the delay is a result of lengthy and often meritless appeals by the convicted person. In some cases, the convicts have had the audacity to suggest that their extended incarceration on death row is, in and of itself, cruel and unusual punishment; and, as such, that their sentences should be commuted. Fortunately, this so called "lackey" defense has failed in most cases, but it shows how opponents of the death penalty, including those sentenced to death, have attempted to use and abuse the court system to achieve something that they cannot achieve in the legislature, and that is the abolition, essentially, of the death penalty.

The reason for their failure to effect change through the normal legislative process is obviously they lack the public support. Public support for the death penalty has remained relatively constant, with approximately 69 percent of Americans in favor of the death penalty and only 24 percent opposed.

My concern here, however, is not for abstract numbers representing the average number of months between sentencing and execution; my concern is for what those numbers mean for the families that have already endured the loss of a loved one and who are forced to endure years and years of prolonged agony as they wait for the justice that the jury has said that they are due.

Three weeks ago, this Committee heard testimony from Mrs. Carol Fornoff, whose 13-year-old daughter Christy was murdered by the maintenance man at an apartment complex near their home in Arizona. The maintenance man was convicted in 1985 of the crime and was sentenced to death. That was 20 years ago. He is still on death row today, having used extensive appeals at both the State and Federal court level to prolong this ordeal for Mrs. Fornoff and her family. I mean, your heart just went out to these people.

Or take the case of a constituent in my district in Cincinnati, Mrs. Sharon Tewskberry. Her husband Monte was stabbed in a convenience store robbery in 1983. Mr. Tewskberry, who was working at the store to make a little extra money to send their daughter to college, managed to crawl outside the store to call his wife from a pay phone after he had been stabbed. She arrived in time to hold him in her arms while he died.

The following year John Byrd, Jr. was convicted of murdering Mr. Tewskberry and was sentenced to die. Nineteen years later, after Byrd had finally exhausted every appeal at both the State and Federal level, including what amounted to a retrial in Federal court of the State law case, John Byrd was finally executed. Nineteen years.

Mr. Chairman, these cases and so many others affirm that justice delayed is justice denied. And there are many, many other cases that I could cite, unfortunately I'm running out of time here. But this is one of the things, since I've been here in Congress, that has been so frustrating. And we passed the Antiterrorism and Effective Death Penalty Act back in 1996, which was supposed to make it a little easier to carry out these sentences, but in practice it's just not worked.

And I would strongly encourage this Committee and the Congress to be serious about this issue, because there are families whose lives have been ripped apart, and they wait and they wait and they wait, and oftentimes 20 years, for justice to be carried out. And we have to make sure that we have an effective enforcement of the death penalty in this country.

And I yield back the balance of my time.

Mr. COBLE. I thank the distinguished gentleman from Ohio.

The Chair recognizes the distinguished gentlelady from Texas, Ms. Jackson Lee, for 5 minutes.

Ms. JACKSON LEE. I thank the distinguished gentleman. To the witnesses, thank you for your presentation. And thank you for the indulgence of other meetings that I had, that I may have not heard the entirety of your testimony. But I do want to acknowledge that this is a very serious issue. And I know that victims are disproportionately sometimes impacted by the system that confuses them that we call justice.

I would only say, without making any frivolous statement, that the alternative to this is to simply take them out and shoot them. We are not that kind of society—that would be expedited, whether we use a firing line, whether we hang them—but that is not the society in which we live.

And so I would just simply say, with the understanding of how we abhor the violent acts that my colleagues have spoken about and the victims that have suffered the rash of sexual predators and killers of children over the last couple of years, however we abhor that, the alternative to a system that we have that allows those charged and convicted the opportunity to pursue their innocence or to pursue their rights in court is a system by which we call democracy and constitutional, I believe.

So it is interesting that we have these discussions about justice being delayed by a period of time. I don't know what the alternative would actually be.

I do want to say to Mr. Marquis that you had in your testimony that you did not believe that one person—or no one could point to one person, single case of a demonstratively innocent person that has been executed in the modern era of American capital punishment. We know that a number of defendants over the years have been proven innocent by DNA.

I would also say by the odds, that we might imagine that there are a number of those in the course of our history, which we would account for the 20th century, particularly knowing the number of African Americans that sit on death row that have gone to their death that certainly have the possibility of being innocent with the proper defense and resources; are you trying to suggest that you can't count one person that you believe was demonstrably innocent that had been executed in modern era?

Mr. MARQUIS. Congresswoman Jackson Lee, if you're talking about post-1976, that is exactly my statement. If you're talking about the 20th century, there is no doubt that innocent people were executed in this country. But we're talking about the post-Gregg era. And more in particularly the last 15 years, because the kinds of due process protections, the kind of counsel—even particularly in your State, as well as others, that have been accorded just in the last 10 or 12 years represent a major improvement.

Ms. JACKSON LEE. Well, I would beg to differ with you. And I'm glad you cited my State.

And Mr. Harcourt, I'm going to ask you a question before the light goes out, so you will be able to answer it before I respond to Mr. Marquis.

In your remarks you said that you answer the proposed bill, the Streamlined Procedures Act of 2005, radical. If I turn the tables on you, they would—opponents of such would presume your statement to be radical. My question to you is, are you radical or are you right? And give us why you assess this bill to be radical, and why you would propose your view to be right.

Let me just comment to him, and I would let you—yield to you to answer.

I really disagree with you on that, because I do live in a State that is notorious for having the highest number of individuals on death row. I venture to say that they have the highest number of executions, and I would venture to say they are predominately minority members, since we happen to predominate on death row anyhow. And we've had a number of cases that have failed as it relates to appropriate counsel, the pardon process—or not the pardon process, but the process of review by our board of review for death penalty cases.

So I would vigorously argue with you whether or not we have complied with due process procedures post-1976. And modern era, as far as I'm concerned, could be considered the 20th century, and certainly could be considered the last half of the 20th century, 1950 and after; and I don't think you can count your comments as accurate.

Mr. Harcourt, could you answer my question about your assessment of the radicalness of this particular bill, and why you're not being radical?

Mr. HARCOURT. Yes——

Mr. COBLE. Professor, the gentlelady's time has expired, but you may answer the question.

Ms. JACKSON LEE. I thank the Chairman for his indulgence.

Mr. HARCOURT. We have to understand that what this bill does is it eliminates Federal habeas corpus in State death penalty cases. That's a—that wasn't done in the AEDPA explicitly. And it eliminates it on one precondition: that the Attorney General of the United States has to certify a State as having competent defense in State post-conviction, and with one extremely narrow elimination, which is slam-dunk evidence of innocence. Basically only DNA would satisfy that.

So what we're talking about is in State death penalty cases, there will not be Federal habeas corpus, okay. I consider that somewhat extreme. It's not what the Congress envisioned with the AEDPA, and I don't think that—I think that it is what one could consider radical.

In addition, eliminating procedural—eliminating cause and prejudice standard for procedural due process in Federal habeas corpus across the board, not just in death penalty cases, but across every single criminal case, you're eliminating the cause and prejudice standard which was created by Chief Justice William Rehnquist in 1977. It was a significant narrowing of the *Faye v. Noya* standard from 1963, which was deliberate bypass, okay, but it was a standard that has been in place, in fact, so much—in place based on federalism and comity concerns, so well engrained in our system of Federal habeas corpus jurisprudence that the AEDPA did not even address procedural due process.

Mr. COBLE. Professor, if you can wrap up. We're all going to have a second round, so you can move along.

Mr. HARCOURT. Thank you, Chairman.

Mr. COBLE. Prior to recognizing the gentleman from Texas, let me remind the Members again that after we adjourn this hearing we will mark up the Secure Access to Justice Bill. So if you all could remain, I would be appreciative.

The Chair recognizes the distinguished gentleman from Texas, Mr. Gohmert, for 5 minutes.

Mr. GOHMERT. Thank you, Mr. Chairman.

With regard to the State of Texas, I do have some experience both as a prosecutor, as a district judge, our highest trial court, and then as an intermediate chief justice of the appellate court.

I had a guy who was nominated for the Federal court by a Democratic President back in the seventies, was nominated for the Fifth Circuit of Appeals, and took that position—by President Clinton. I had him speak to a Rotary Club some years back and he said, on being asked during question and answer what do you think about the death penalty in Texas, and his words were—and he's much more moderate than I am—but he said, you don't have the death penalty in Texas. And people began to get all ruffled. And he said, if you're waiting 10 to 20 years to put somebody to death, and do it in the middle of the night when nobody can see and nobody can be around, you don't really have the death penalty.

Interestingly enough, there's something to his comments. We have put people to death. I do challenge anybody to show since 1976—I don't know about before then, I wasn't licensed before then—but anyone who had been executed since that time who was innocent.

I know there were a lot of people who have been guilty who have had cases reversed. I get sick and tired of hearing people say that, well, you know, we know in Texas they didn't get proper representation because defense attorneys are not on the proper level with the seasoned prosecutors.

I had never tried a murder, I had never tried a death penalty case, and yet in 1986 I was appointed to appeal a capital murder conviction, and I did one fantastic job because I worked my tail off. And there was not proper due process in the trial and it was reversed.

So I get a little sick of saying that somebody like me was not competent in the appeal of a death penalty case. I have tried them as a trial judge. And for those who don't know, it's not enough to be convicted of capital murder, as Mr. Lungren pointed out, you have a bifurcated trial, and then go into—in Texas it's basically three questions that in essence say, number one, did you commit the murder or know that the murder was going to be committed; number two, are you a future danger; and number three, is there anything whatsoever that mitigates against getting the death penalty? And man, that opens the door to all kinds of testimony. And only if you get a yes, yes, no is the judge in a position to pronounce a death penalty.

Also in the issue of race, my anecdotal situation, I understand what the numbers are statewide. I had three people convicted of capital murder in my court in a decade, and two of them got the death penalty. They were both white, and the one that didn't was an African American.

With regard to this issue of studies, I'd like to ask, do any of the four of you know of any studies about recidivism or the deterrence effect of capital murder sentences that were done before the modern era of habeas corpus in cases taking 10 to 20 years? Do any of you know of any studies before we started dragging death penalty 10 to 20 years——

Mr. HARCOURT. Your Honor——

Mr. COBLE. The red light is about to illuminate, but you all may answer.

Mr. HARCOURT. Thank you.

The original studies about deterrence were done in the early 1970's, and that was the Erlich study, which had originally suggested that there was deterrence, but it was subjected to a lot of review; and ultimately an expert panel of the National Academy of Sciences issued a strong criticism of the early study. And I think that that would cover a period of where it was not prolonged death penalty appeals and processes. So the evidence there suggested no deterrence.

Mr. GOHMERT. Okay. Let me just ask you—and I appreciate what I believe is your great candor, Mr. Harcourt. You mentioned 12 death penalty cases in a discussion about proof beyond a reasonable doubt of innocence. In those 12 cases, was there proof beyond a reasonable doubt of innocence, or just some procedural flaw or reasonable doubt such that created no additional trial after reversal?

Mr. HARCOURT. Those 12 cases were referring to 12 DNA exonerations in death penalty cases; exonerations, meaning wrong person. The blood—the blood or semen or whatever other human cells that were obtained and checked for DNA purposes were a different person. So those would be 12 DNA exonerations.

Of course the other cases of approximately more than 100 exonerations or cases of actual innocence don't involve DNA. And so as a result of that, what I'm suggesting is, of course, there is always lingering debate because you don't have rock-solid proof, and it's——

Mr. GOHMERT. And is it possible that the DNA, the so-called exoneration may just have raised such doubt that that person could have been there, knowing the crime was going to be committed, but it's just that with the DNA evidence it created a reasonable doubt that wasn't worth trying?

Mr. HARCOURT. Well——

Mr. COBLE. The gentleman's time has expired. You can respond tersely.

Mr. HARCOURT. Right. Well, these are cases where Governors in most cases have exonerated individuals on the belief, firm belief, that they were not the individuals who committed the crime.

Mr. GOHMERT. Thank you. Thank you, Mr. Chairman.

Mr. COBLE. I thank the gentleman. Now we are coming up to another vote before too long, but I think a second vote is warranted, so we will move along. And I appreciate the panelists hanging tough as you have.

I'll start the second round.

Mr. Sabin, since 9/11 the impact of terrorism has become a regular experience with most Americans now that was virtually unknown prior to 9/11. But in the death penalty framework, Mr. Sabin, why are terrorist offenses treated not unlike treason and espionage cases rather than traditional homicides?

Mr. SABIN. The threat and harm to society that is prevalent in the present statutory framework for treason and espionage cases is in the same vein as would be in terrorism cases; the fact, as we have discussed earlier, that there is a grave risk to society based upon the threat that thousands, tens of thousands of people could be killed by that act of treason or by that act of espionage or by that act of terrorism, rather than a specific murder that occurs. So under section 101 of the proposed legislation, you would have terrorist offenses that result in death.

And the other section of the proposed legislation, you would have terrorism put on that same playing field as treason or espionage cases because of the widespread impact upon society.

Mr. COBLE. I thank you, Mr. Sabin.

Mr. Marquis, with the passage—we may have gotten into this previously, but I want to extend it one more time.

With the passage of the Justice for All Act and creation of post-conviction DNA testing procedures, what impact will that have upon addressing concerns of innocent defendants on death row?

Mr. MARQUIS. In response to, I think, one of the comments by—I think it may have been the Congresswoman from Texas, the idea that we are conducting summary proceedings could not be farther from the truth. I have one person that I have put on death row. He committed his murders in 1987; we're about to have the fourth trial for him.

To be blunt, in the United States, defendants are—in death penalty cases, are drowned in due process. And that probably is the way it should be; if we're seeking to take someone's life, that's very important. The reason that these cases go on at such length is because almost universally now, a very high level of lawyer is provided.

In my State, which is not atypical, there have to be at least two; you have to be death qualified, you have to have previously tried a murder case. And I did death penalty defense, and I was able to do it because I had previously tried a murder case.

In my State we spend more money on indigent defense all over, not just in capital cases, than we do on prosecution. That's not the case everywhere in the United States. But I think it's important to note that, particularly with the passage of Justice for All Act, one of the concerns was, well, what if somebody—if there is a new DNA case and it comes up later?

As a prosecutor it is my worst nightmare that I would prosecute an innocent person. And I don't believe there should be any block against bringing up evidence at any point in a proceeding, no matter where you are procedurally, if the person really didn't do it.

Mr. COBLE. And I concur with that.

Mr. Eisenberg, this may be duplicating. I don't think we've addressed this specifically. What is your view of a proposal to scale back Federal review at the district court and appellate levels? And how well situated are State judges in vindicating Federal constitutional rights?

Mr. EISENBERG. Mr. Chairman, we are certainly facing delays at both of those levels of the Federal courts. The only level in which cases move at a reasonable predictable pace is if and when they ever get to the United States Supreme Court, which is extremely rare.

In the district courts, I mentioned one case in my written testimony, hasn't gotten an appeal yet, it's still in the district court where it has been kicking around for I think 4 years now. And just a couple of weeks ago the judge issued an order in the case, but the order is not a decision on the case; that's just an order setting oral argument about all the briefs that had been filed so far.

So it has taken us 4 years to get to the point where the district judge ordered oral argument, which is supposed to take place next month—who knows how many years until he finally rules? And only then will we even start the appeals.

In State court, of course, these cases are getting judicial attention much earlier. And as I mentioned previously, there are many State courts that have reversed many death penalty cases. Now, that's been argued by some as proving that there are all these errors in these cases. But if that's true, if we can rely on those State court judgments, we can certainly rely on the State court judgments that affirm death penalty cases as well.

Mr. COBLE. Well, when you said district court, you meant Federal district court?

Mr. EISENBERG. Yes. I meant the lower level of the Federal courts, which happens after all the State court appeals; the first thing that happens in Federal court.

Mr. COBLE. I thank you, sir.

The distinguished gentleman from Virginia is recognized for 5 minutes.

Mr. SCOTT. Thank you.

Mr. Marquis, you indicated if someone has evidence that they're innocent, they ought to be heard and have that opportunity. If it's—if you have evidence that's not DNA evidence, what kind of chance would you have if you were factually innocent?

Mr. MARQUIS. Well, there are—in addition to the various direct appeals, Federal appeals, habeas appeals, if there is evidence of innocence. This is where there is something, some amount of the human factor. Evidence is brought to prosecutors and to Governors, and it is not uncommon in this country for prosecutors——

Mr. SCOTT. If you can convince the prosecutor. But if the prosecutor doesn't want to go along, what can you present to a judge under these bills that will allow you to be heard?

Mr. MARQUIS. I can't speak to what can be provided under these bills——

Mr. SCOTT. Well, under present law you don't have much because you've got to have evidence of—clear and convincing evidence to get past a motion, frivolous charge. I mean, you've got to show clear and convincing evidence. If all you've got is evidence that you're probably innocent, do you get a hearing?

Mr. MARQUIS. I think it requires more than that.

Mr. SCOTT. Right, okay.

If under H.R. 3035, Professor Harcourt, if a State court has ruled that the evidence—that the error was harmless, can the Federal court review that finding?

Mr. HARCOURT. Not on a sentencing issue, Congressman Scott. One of the provisions of H.R. 3035—I think it's specifically provision 6, section 6—suggests that if a State court, in post-conviction or on direct appeal, finds that a claim regarding a sentence or a sentencing process—this applies whether it's a death penalty case or an ordinary criminal case—if the sentencing claim is harmless or that they found out it was not prejudicial in some way, then the claim cannot be reviewed in Federal habeas corpus.

Mr. SCOTT. Is that the same for ineffective counsel?

Mr. HARCOURT. Well, that's precisely the point. Ineffective assistance of counsel is a two-prong standard that requires inadequate—or performance that's not up to par. And then prejudice. It's a two-prong standard which has a prejudice prong in it. So effectively, any kinds of claims of ineffective assistance of counsel regarding sentencing—which, of course, some of the most significant kind of cases that we see—in fact, the United States Supreme Court has just reversed a few cases because of inadequate counsel at the sentencing phase—would be barred by this legislation.

Mr. SCOTT. Now, if you haven't exhausted State remedies and you file your petition in Federal court, do I understand this bill to say it is dismissed with prejudice?

Mr. HARCOURT. Correct.

Mr. SCOTT. That means when you go back to State court, you can't come back.

Mr. HARCOURT. That's correct. Under present AEDPA law—actually in a ruling just issued this year by the United States Supreme Court in *Ryans v. Webber,* and under the AEDPA, there is essentially some discretion provided to Federal judges in cases of unexhausted claims. It's a very limited discretion.

Mr. SCOTT. They can dismiss it without prejudice, or they can hold it until you've been there.

Mr. HARCOURT. Correct. Although it's very limited. I mean, you have to show that you're likely to prevail, et cetera. It's not as if it would apply to all unexhausted——

Mr. SCOTT. But if they dismiss it, it wouldn't be with prejudice, so you could never bring it back.

Mr. HARCOURT. Correct, yes.

Mr. SCOTT. My time is almost over. I had a couple of quick questions.

Under H.R. 3060, when a jury has found someone guilty but can't decide on the—or is hung on the question of guilt, the bill provides for a new jury to come in on the question of death—a new jury to come in.

Has a court ever reviewed what happens if a jury cannot unanimously decide death? I thought the rule was that you have to impose life, is it——

Mr. EISENBERG. May I address that, Congressman? We did have a case from my State that I believe touched on this issue and went up to the United States Supreme Court. And the United States Supreme Court held that, in fact, if the sentencing jury can't decide on death, that's not a double jeopardy bar to retrying the issue.

There are some States which by statute don't allow another sentencing hearing, which automatically impose a life sentence in the event of a hung jury.

Mr. SCOTT. Do you have a case on that specific point? Could we get the name of that?

Mr. SABIN. I believe it's the Jones case.

Mr. SCOTT. Which said if the jury is hung on that question, it is not double jeopardy to come back. So if we change the statute, then that case would answer the question on constitutionality of that provision.

Mr. SABIN. I don't think it quite held that that was the holding. I believe there was not unanimity. There were questions about the jury instructions and whether you had to impose death, life sentence, or another sentence that would be less than death. And the confusion that was suggested created in the jury by those instructions impacted upon the court's decision.

Mr. SCOTT. Okay. And the other question is, there is a provision to proceed with less than 12 jurors in H.R. 3060. Does anybody want to comment on that, and whether courts have reviewed going forward on a death penalty case with less than 12 jurors over the objection of the defense?

Mr. COBLE. The gentleman's time has expired, but you may answer.

Mr. SABIN. I don't believe a court has held in that regard; that is correct. If good cause is found, a judge under this proposed bill can proceed with a jury of less than 12 without the defendant's stipulation.

Mr. SCOTT. And has any court—and no court has ruled on that as a denial of due process; is that right?

Mr. SABIN. I am not aware of court proceedings. We can get back to you on that of any specific court, if the Supreme Court or lower level has reviewed that.

Mr. COBLE. The gentleman's time has expired. The distinguished gentleman from California is recognized for 5 minutes.

Mr. LUNGREN. Thank you, Mr. Chairman.

Mr. Harcourt, you correctly noted in your testimony that the current law allows a State to trigger a special set of more advantageous, as you say, to the State procedural rules for Federal habeas corpus proceedings if the State establishes an effective system providing competent counsel to indigents in State post-conviction proceedings. You also note that Federal courts determine whether a State scheme for supplying counsel meets the statutory criteria, and this is the so-called opt-in feature of AEDPA. But then you then criticized the bill I have introduced for placing the decision of whether the State qualifies for chapter 154 treatment in the hands of the U.S. Attorney General. You contend this: A State that gets something, advantageous procedural rules in Federal court in exchange for doing something, providing good lawyers to indigents in State proceedings, this section would change both ends of that quid pro quo equation.

Look, I know that many States, including my own, have devoted great effort and expense toward providing the type of counsel that chapter 154 requires. As a matter of fact, when we drafted the law California was used as the model. But it has now been 9 years since the passage of the law, can you name me one State that has been permitted by the Federal Courts of Appeals to qualify for chapter 154? And hasn't the quid pro quo equation under current law that you celebrate effectively always meant a zero for the State side of the equation?

Mr. HARCOURT. If I'm not mistaken, I believe that Arizona qualified for the opt-in provisions under the Ninth Circuit review. And I believe that's the—I believe that is the only State that has qualified for the opt-in procedures.

Mr. LUNGREN. Does it sound like it's working?

Mr. HARCOURT. Well, the question is whether adequate counsel is being provided in State post-conviction proceedings.

Mr. LUNGREN. That's true. And it's interesting that we modeled that section after the California experience, and yet the courts have not found that to be appropriate; thereby, it looks like, ignoring what we tried to suggest was appropriate.

I have so many questions here. Let me ask you this. You criticize section 14 of the bill, which you say would overrule the U.S. Supreme Court's interpretation of the 1996 act as not applying to pending claims. And today, 9 years after the law was enacted, a small but significant number of habeas corpus petitions still remain that were not governed by it and are still subject to the pre-1996 standards. You state in your testimony that legislatively overruling the Supreme Court's interpretation and applying it to all current cases would trigger massive litigation over whether the U.S. Constitution allows Congress to do this.

Now, the Lynn case, 1997, the Supreme Court that held that the 1996 law did not apply to pending cases, was a 5–4 decision. Are you aware of any passage in either the majority decision or the dissent in that case, that suggests that Congress could not have applied AEDPA to pending claims? And if applying them to pending petitions would have raised such constitutional concerns, don't you think that at least one justice would have mentioned this?

Mr. HARCOURT. Congressman, I don't have the Lynn decision right in front of me, so I can't quote any language from it, but I believe there was a claim raised as to the retroactive application of new procedures in that case, which would be precisely the kind of constitutional claim that would be raised as a result of this H.R. 3035, if the—part of the bill provides that it applies to cases that are pending right now.

Mr. LUNGREN. You also suggest that many sections of the legislation would raise significant constitutional questions about the prior Congress to restrict Federal court review of habeas claims, including whether or not the bill violates the suspension clause of the United States Constitution. You later assert that the bill would arguably suspend the writ of habeas corpus.

In the Lynn case, the court of appeals described the constitutionally guaranteed writ of habeas corpus this way: The writ known in 1789 was the pretrial contest of the Executive's power to hold a person captive, the device that prevents arbitrary detention without trial. The power thus enshrined did not include the ability to reexamine judgments rendered by courts possessing jurisdiction. Under the original practice, the judgment of conviction rendered by the court of general criminal jurisdiction was the conclusive proof that confinement was legal and prevented issuance of a writ. The founding area of historical evidence suggests a prevailing view that State courts were adequate fora for protecting Federal rights. Based on this assumption, there was, and is, no constitutionally enshrined right to mount a collateral attack on a State court's judgment in the inferior article 3 courts, and, a fortiori, no mandate that State court judgments embracing questionable or even erroneous interpretations of the Federal Constitution be reviewed by the interior article 3 courts.

The Seventh Circuit then concluded: Any suggestion that the Constitution forbids every contraction of the habeas power bestowed by the Congress in 1885 and expanded by the 1948 and 1996 amendments is untenable.

My question is, do you think that the Ninth Circuit got it wrong?

Mr. COBLE. The gentleman's time has expired.

Mr. LUNGREN. I talked as fast as I could.

Mr. COBLE. I'm not admonishing you, but you may respond to that, Professor.

Mr. HARCOURT. Thank you, Chairman.

The question of constitutionality here has to do with whether or not you can grant Federal jurisdiction to a Federal court up to a certain point where a violation of Federal law would be discovered, okay, but at which point the jurisdiction would be stripped, and so the court couldn't do anything. So that's probably the most complicated constitutional issue that this statute presents. In other words, it would be a situation where a Federal district court would be able to—would see a violation of Federal law, but would not be able to—but then jurisdiction would be stripped right at that point because the lower court found it harmless or because there is no procedural default rules in place anymore, et cetera.

What really becomes questionable with H.R. 3035 is that point where jurisdiction is stripped after a Federal court would have found a substantive violation of a Federal constitutional right.

Mr. LUNGREN. So you think the Seventh Circuit got it wrong.

Mr. HARCOURT. You were talking about the Ninth Circuit.

Mr. LUNGREN. Seventh Circuit. I agree with you, the Ninth Circuit gets it wrong often, but I'm talking about the Seventh Circuit in this case.

Mr. HARCOURT. Right. I don't think that in that particular case, the Seventh Circuit was addressing the constitutional issue that H.R. 3035 raises.

Mr. COBLE. The gentleman's time is expired. And I say to my friend from California, I was not admonishing you because you were speaking at an accelerated rate, you were trying to beat that red light.

Mr. LUNGREN. It may be difficult for you to understand from North Carolina, but we do talk a little faster out where I come from. Thank you.

Mr. COBLE. We have been joined by the distinguished gentleman from Florida, Mr. Keller.

Now I ask my friends on the majority side, does anyone have any question on the second round?

Mr. Keller, the gentleman from Florida.

Mr. KELLER. Thank you, Mr. Chairman. And I apologize for not being here on the first round.

Having read the powerful testimony, I just wonder if our Ranking Member, Mr. Scott, is now persuaded to be in support of the death penalty. And I will yield.

Mr. SCOTT. Nice try, Mr.——

Mr. KELLER. I will yield back the balance of my time then.

Mr. COBLE. The gentleman yields back the balance of his time.

And I want to thank the Members who have stayed with us throughout the entire hearing. And I want to express my thanks to the very distinguished panelists and those in the audience who have attended very dutifully. The Subcommittee appreciates your contribution.

In order to ensure a full record and adequate consideration of this important issue, the record will be left open for additional submissions for seven days. Also, any written questions that a Member wants to submit should be submitted within the same seven-day period.

This concludes the legislative hearing on, "Does an Accurate and Swift Death Penalty Deter Crime And Save Lives: H.R. 3060, the "Terrorist Death Penalty Enhancement Act of 2005;" and H.R. 3035, the "Streamlined Procedures Act of 2005."

We will now proceed with the markup—without objection, the hearing is adjourned and we will proceed with the markup of H.R. 1751, the "Secure Access to Justice and Court Protection Act of 2005."

Again, I say to the panelists, thank you so much, gentlemen, for being with us.

[Whereupon, at 4:20 p.m., the Subcommittee proceeded to other business.]

APPENDIX

MATERIAL SUBMITTED FOR THE HEARING RECORD

LETTER FROM MICHAEL ISRAEL, EDITOR, *CRIMINAL JUSTICE WASHINGTON LETTER,* TO THE HONORABLE HOWARD COBLE, A REPRESENTATIVE IN CONGRESS FROM THE STATE OF NORTH CAROLINA, AND CHAIRMAN, SUBCOMMITTEE ON CRIME, TERRORISM, AND HOMELAND SECURITY, AND THE HONORABLE ROBERT C. SCOTT, A REPRESENTATIVE IN CONGRESS FROM THE STATE OF VIRGINIA, AND RANKING MEMBER, SUBCOMMITTEE ON CRIME, TERRORISM, AND HOMELAND SECURITY

June 29, 2005

The Honorable Howard Coble
Chair, Subcommittee on Crime, Terrorism and Homeland Security
2468 RHOB
United States House of Representatives
Washington, D.C. 20515

The Honorable Bobby Scott
Ranking Member, Subcommittee on Crime, Terrorism and Homeland Security
1201 LHOB
United States House of Representatives
Washington, D.C. 20515

Dear Reps. Coble and Scott,

I am taking the liberty to write one letter for the record on two bills scheduled for hearings June 30, 2005: HR 3060, The Death Penalty Enhancement Act of 2005, and HR 3035, The Streamlined procedures Act of 2005. I bring to this discussion a 36 year academic career as a criminologist, and familiarity with the empirical research on the functional consequences of the death penalty, and 25 years as an advisor to a group of prisoners known as The Lifers Group in Rahway Prison in New Jersey, many of whom were serving their sentences for what would have been capitol murder had there been such a state statute at the time.

As for HR 3060, there is no reason for me to repeat the arguments of the June 17 memo from the ACLU, except to add my perspective from my experience as a social scientist and one who has worked with incarcerated murderers. The following are my responses to arguments in support of the bill:

No innocent person has been executed, as far as we know: But many innocent people have been convicted, and we know this from irrefutable DNA evidence. The Innocence Project has exonerated approximately 150 wrongly convicted persons, and "exonerated" does not mean legally reversed. They spent many years in prison, and they will carry mental scars for their lifetime. Aside from arguments on what is the "error rate," percentages in this case are less important for public policy than the absolute number of 150. No one would support a public policy with 150 wrongfully executed, and nothing that their states did would have discovered those errors.

There is a public interest in permanent incapacitation: There certainly is, and there are some dangerous predators that should be in prison for life. One pro death penalty argument is that without its finality, many years down the road murderers will eventually get out and prey on the public. Aside from the life-without-parole alternative, a reality check is that the majority of capital murderers are not career criminals or repeat predators, and in fact murderers represent the best chance for rehabilitation. Most are dysfunctional individuals who acted on impulse, and at an elderly age the chance of repeating their crime is negligible. I am not recommending parole for heinous murderers, but in the event there is a commutation years later, the public interest is not threatened.

Victims' families want closure: They certainly do, but it is a myth that families of murder victims all want the death penalty. Closure means they want the case adjudicated and over with. Prosecutors seeking death is the worst way to achieve that, for the case will last for years and questions about its justice will remain forever. A life sentence will bring closure for victims in a shorter time, with far less looking back.

"**Super due process" will protect the innocent in terrorism cases:** From my experience, I fear the opposite. High profile capital cases—and the mere word "terrorism" will put any case on Court TV—bringing with them enormous pressure to convict. I can't imagine any jury walking out of an American courthouse having found anyone accused of a capitol related terrorism case not guilty, and expect to go on with their lives as before. The 150 exonerated DNA cases all had super due process.

Furthermore, every member of the defense bar who has represented a capitol client on appeals knows the unwritten law in that environment: it's not enough to argue law, but a substantial case for innocence must be made. Appellate judges will not over rule a high profile capitol conviction on due process issues alone, but if they want any kind of future in the law and as members of their communities they must satisfy the court of public opinion, sitting in the courtroom of Court TV and the 24 hour popular news media, that they saved the life of someone for whom the judicial system made an error of fact.

This brings me to HR 3035, if you will permit me to discuss two bills in one letter. Again I refer to the environment for the defense bar in high profile, heinous murder cases, both criminal and terrorism related. We all know that in many instances this extremely difficult work is largely done by volunteer lawyers. They rarely can commit their full time energies to these cases, and they work on them on weekends and late at night. For them, the time limits in this bill are unreasonable. As a practical matter this bill goes a long way toward denial of vigorous counsel in the cases where it may be needed most.

Every defense lawyer knows that the hardest win, by far, in the entire post conviction process, and also the rarest win, is by federal habeas corpus. This bill addresses a problem that does not exist. The Supreme Court did much to close the door in Wainwright v. Sykes on 1977. In rare cases, however, the last chance, the one final place to take a hysteria fueled case out of the pressure that goes with terrorism cases is federal habeas corpus. That "last chance" ought to be preserved.

Very truly yours,

Michael Israel, Pd.D.
Editor, Criminal Justice Washington Letter
5505 Connecticut Ave., NW
Box 300
Washington, D.C. 20015-2601
Phone: 301-270-5944
Fax: 301-270-5966

○